THE LORI FACTOR

Live the Life You Were
Born to Live

LORI BRUTON

Foreword by Les Brown

Copyright © 2021 by Lori Bruton
Published by Lori Bruton in Partnership with
Bold Publishing
(https://denisenicholson.com/bold-publishing)

Book Cover by: Opeyemi Ikuborije
Book Layout by: Opeyemi Ikuborije

Publisher's Note:

Without limiting the rights under copyright reserved above, no part of this publication may be reproduced, stored in or introduced into a retrieval system, or transmitted, in any form, or by any means (electronic, mechanical, photocopying, recording, or otherwise), without the prior written permission of both the copyright owner and the publisher of the book.

Manufactured in the United States of America

ISBN: 978-1-7363853-4-0

Library of Congress Control Number: 20211918287

Follow Lori Bruton
Social Media Outlets:

Facebook: @ LoriBrutonbiz

Instagram: @ loribrutonbiz

LinkedIn: https://www.linkedin.com/in/loribrutonbiz

Twitter: https://www.twitter.com/loribruton

Youtube: https://bit.ly/lorisstories

Pinterest: https://www.pinterest.com/lbessentials4u/

CONTENTS

Testimonials . . . . *vi*

Dedication . . . . *viii*

Acknowledgments. . . . .*x*

Foreword. . . . . *xii*

Preface . . . . *xiv*

Introduction: *Who Am I and Why Should You Care?*. 1

CHAPTER 1. 3

    L = LARGER *Larger vision of yourself beyond your circumstances* . . . 3

    LOVE - *What's Love Got to Do with It?*. 8

    LEVERAGE - *A Favor to Your Success*. 12

    LIFESTYLE - *Start Living Life on Your Terms*. 15

    LEGACY - *Live a Life That Outlives You*. 18

CHAPTER 2 21

O = OPTIMISM *A favorable outlook and belief you can change your life* 21

OVERCOMER - *Bust Through Obstacles* 23

OPEN - *Keep Your Heart and Mind Open to the Truth* 26

OBEDIENCE - *An Act of Faith* 31

OPPORTUNITIES - *Right Opportunities Change Lives* 33

CHAPTER 3 35

R = REINVENT *Yourself* 35

RISKS - *Success requires Sacrifice.* 42

RESPONSIBILITY - *Break Up with Self-Sabotage and Reclaim Your Power* 44

RICH - *What Does "RICH" Mean to You?* 48

RADIANCE - *Let Your Light Shine* 51

CHAPTER 4 53

I = INVEST *in Yourself.* 53

INITIATIVE - *Ready, Set, Go.* 55

INTENTIONAL - *Make Things Happen* 57

LIVE INTENTIONALLY WITH URGENCY 59

IDENTITY - *Do You Know Who You Are?* 63

YOU ARE A GEM - *A Valuable Treasure* 64

INFLUENCE - *Are you being affected or "infected" by Influencers?* .66

CHAPTER 5 69

YOU ARE ENOUGH = *Embrace HIS Greatness* *69*
STORY OF ESTHER - *Transformation and Transition* *71*
SUPPER TIME - *Eat This Bread* *74*
GET DRUNK - *A Different Kind of Intoxication* *77*

CHAPTER 6 81

YOUR VISION = *See, Believe, Act* *81*

CHAPTER 7 85

NEXT STEPS - *Choose Your Path* *85*

TESTIMONIALS

Lori is known as the Queen of Hope, but to me, Lori is the Reinvention Queen. Lori is quiet and at first might appear unassuming. Beneath her quiet demeanor lies a woman of steel. Lori is on a mission to use her gifts, her passion, her story, and combine these with her wisdom and experience and share with the world, a powerful message of hope, inspiration, and resilience. In this inspirational book, Lori shares her transformational journey from breakdown to breakthrough, from self-doubt to self-worth, from despair to deliverance. She shares the pivotal moment when she had an awakening and went from powerless to purposeful.

Lori has a powerful message, and it is no wonder why Les Brown, as soon as he heard it, offered to write the Foreword. Great job, Lori! Lori personifies power, hope, and resilience.

For anyone who needs words of hope, encouragement, motivation, and inspiration (who doesn't?) this book is a must read. It will change lives. I am immensely proud and honored to call Lori my friend.

~ Ene Obi

Lori is one of the most amazing, talented, smart, and beautiful women of God. She has impacted my life in so many ways. She showed compassion when I shared my story. We bonded after that because Lori listens to details very well. I am so glad God brought us together. Lori changed my life in many ways. I greatly appreciate her hard work and dedication.

~ Catherine Mitchell

Lori Bruton is the epitome of resilience and perseverance. When life doesn't always go the way she wants it to, she remains unstoppable. Those qualities serve her readers well when she takes them on the journey of transformation and growth. She models behavior for others that is inspiring. I highly recommend keeping your eye on Lori for the next glimpse of inspiration.

~ Sheila Kennedy

I am Kasundra "Dr. K." Brown: The Tilted Fedora Trainer, motivational teacher, inspirational speaker, author, and transformational thought coach. It is with great enthusiasm that I recommend Lori Bruton to anyone who wants to develop a *L*arger vision of themselves, become *O*ptimistic in their mindset, *R*einvent themselves to become what they are created to be and *I*nvest in themselves in a way that will return marvelous dividends. Lori's story is inspiring and uplifting. She speaks encouragement and hope into the lives of everyone she meets. Her book, the LORI Factor will change lives and empower readers around the globe to live their best lives and be their best selves. Her desire and capacity to serve from the heart will impact others at an awe-inspiring level. It is a true pleasure to be connected to someone who speaks, writes, and presents from a place of true authenticity. I am honored to call her my friend.

~ Kasundra "Dr. K" Brown

DEDICATION

I dedicate this book to Les Brown, my mentor, who has helped me to develop the idea and story of *The LORI Factor*. Les, thank you for believing in me, and for bringing my story to life. Now it can impact many as you have greatly impacted me. It's a fun fact that we both have the initials LB.

I dedicate this book not only to my earthly father, but also to my heavenly Father, who filled me with an entrepreneurial spirit, and gave me the courage and belief that I can do anything I put my mind to. Thank you for giving me life, and filling me with hope, faith, love, and joy.

I dedicate this book to my son, Kevin, a man of leadership and influence. He has touched many lives, especially mine. I am grateful for him and his loving, loyal wife, Tina. Kevin, you give the best hugs, and you make me laugh. Every moment with you is a treasure. Tina, thank you for loving my son. I appreciate you both. Love you always and forever.

I dedicate this book to my friends, family, and colleagues who took time for me, prayed for me, cheered me on, and provided opportunities needed. Thank you for listening, and thanks for all that you have taught me.

I dedicate this book to all my writing mentors and colleagues who encouraged me to keep going, keep writing; and helped me hone my skill and message. Thank you for also helping with the publication, and getting it into the hands of those who have been eagerly waiting.

I dedicate this book to you, who will read and receive the message that was put on my heart to share. May these words stir up your greatness and enrich your life abundantly, so that you can live the life you were born to live.

ACKNOWLEDGMENTS

The LORI Factor would have been aborted if not for these brilliant minds. It truly takes a dream team to bring a dream into reality. My name now makes a statement and expresses a powerful message thanks to all these powerful people.

Gary Coxe, calling me onto your stage and helping me identify where I was, how I got there, and where I wanted to go was a defining moment. It brought me to the decision to end a toxic relationship. It was the grand finale of that event, but a new beginning for me. I am in a better place because of you. Thank you. Full throttle, Baby!

Manny Lopez, thank you for inviting me into your Network of Influence, connecting me with amazing people such as yourself. Serving your way to success is a principle everyone needs to practice. You helped me achieve a higher level which gives me the opportunity to be an influencer and thought leader.

John-Leslie Brown, the day we met you saw something special in me that I could not see in myself. Your loving support, training, and guiding my steps helped me step into my dream of accomplishing author status and that my story matters. You said we would change lives together. Thanks for welcoming me with love and open arms into your family. We are family. Much love and gratitude to you.

Les Brown, you saw my heart from the start. Without you, there would be a missing piece in my heart. You showed me how to break my silence and develop my power voice. It's an ongoing journey. I found the courage and determination to tell my story so that it can impact and save lives. I am thankful for our Divine connection. What an honor that you wrote the Foreword for this book and that you germinated the seed of *The LORI Factor*. Now we can watch it grow together. Thank you for taking time for me and this important work. Hugs and love.

Denise Nicholson, *(https://denisenicholson.com/bold-publishing)* our connection was meant to be. Thank you for accepting me where I was. Thank you for your time, investment, patience, and love in getting my story told and published. Writing this book was a healing journey for me, and I believe it will be a healing journey to those who read it and will add value to their lives. You and your team are amazing. I appreciate the expertise it took to birth this work of art. Love you.

Joseph and Stefanie Bruton, my dear son and daughter-in-love. **Joe**, this mother's heart is overflowing with gratitude that you love me through good times and bad. We have been through challenging times. You never left my side. When you found your wonderful wife, our family became richer. **Stefanie**, you are a treasure and a joy. You both get me. I would not have made it this far without you both. I appreciate you more than you know. Many blessings to you. God brought me blessings and joy having you both in my life. Love you always and forever.

Daddy, you are absolutely good. Your love is the deepest and truest of all time. You never gave up on me even when I gave up on myself. You always keep your promises. You never leave me. We have cried together, laughed together, danced together, have shared deep conversations and more. Thank you for the gifts of writing, speaking, love and compassion. May our journey continue for eternity. Thanks for creating me for a purpose. It is an honor to share You with others so that we can expand our family. I'll never let go. Keep holding my hand. Bless You, Father God.

FOREWORD

You have something special, you have GREATNESS in YOU!

If you have followed my career or heard me speak, then you know that I believe that each of us was born with special and unique gifts that we need to share with the world.

In fact, I believe that if or when you do not share your greatness with others, the rest of us suffer. Yes, it's true… you are that powerful, and so is your purpose.

I can't tell you how relieved I am that after decades of searching for what I was put here to do, that I finally found… and USED my gifts.

Have you? If not, don't feel ashamed. There is still time for you, just like there was for me, but you've got to be determined and HUNGRY to make it.

If you have found your purpose in life but have gotten off track for any reason, that's okay too. Life happens to all of us: the most important thing to know is that it's possible for you to turn it all around. That's why I'm glad that you've found this book.

The L.O.R.I. Factor is a great "how to" guide to find your way in life.

Lori Bruton shares her story of overcoming painful events and depression: learning to see a Larger vision of herself by using Optimism to Reinvent, and Invest in herself to turn her life around, and start winning. She shows how you can do the same. I appreciate Lori's honesty, openness, and transparency in this book.

If you are seeking direction and looking for a way to transform your life, keep reading! *The **LORI** Factor* will show you the way.

That's my story, and I'm sticking to it

Yours in GREATNESS,

Les Brown

Speaker, Author, Trainer

PREFACE

This book has the potential to become the avenue to your miracle. It gives insights and examples of experiences I've been through that can enlighten and encourage you. Yes, it may entertain you but beyond that, let it give you hope and reveal truths that you may not have known or considered.

No matter what you believe or what you've been through, these pages can uncover treasures you have yet to discover. It's no accident that you have this book in your hands. I wrote this with love. Come with an open mind and heart. Let this message not merely inform you but transform you.

It's time to speak up, be bold, and let my voice be heard, because staying silent cannot help anyone. I speak new, empowering life over you and into you, dear one. My life was spared and saved so that I can give you hope and make a difference in your life. It is my honor to do so.

Enjoy reading my story. May it touch your heart in a special way.

INTRODUCTION

Who Am I and Why Should You Care?

I'll Start Here: Who I Was and Who I Am Now

I used to be known as "Quiet Little Lori" and felt invisible for many years growing up. Later, I got married and had two wonderful sons. Life was good, until… my past that I had buried resurrected and came bursting out of me, causing a breakdown and great loss; mostly of myself. I went down a dangerous path and made shocking, destructive decisions that resulted in guilt, shame, self-sabotage, and self-hatred.

Thankfully, *that Lori* no longer exists: I reinvented myself. I am not defined by my past and neither are you. I am here for you. Let my story encourage and inspire you to be who you were created to be.

This book is for those who want to get unstuck and get more out of life. It is for those who feel hopeless, brokenhearted, unloved, and unsure of their purpose: those who want motivation, inspiration, hope, truth, transformation, and choose to live life to the fullest.

Let me walk you through **The LORI Factor**:

L = LARGER vision of yourself beyond your circumstances.

O = OPTIMISM -- the possibility that you can change your life.

R = REINVENT yourself--how to make a radical change in your life.

I = INVEST in yourself.

Beyond those main key points, I dive deeper into this framework in each section by giving you not only the meaning of each letter, but also giving you more pieces to this word puzzle. Words can speak life, depending on which words you speak. Now you have tools to discover the missing pieces of your personal puzzle, and the know-how to put them together. I share life-changing truths from my own experiences as well as from the #1 best-selling motivational book of all time. If you don't know what I'm talking about; stay tuned.

What's in it for you?

You will walk away with a larger vision and deeper love for yourself. Your identity, purpose, and calling may be revealed. You will gain the optimism and belief of doing more, achieving more, knowing that it's possible. You will emerge into who you want to be as you learn new beliefs, behaviors, and strategies. You have already invested in yourself by being here. You will develop the confidence, clarity, and passion to do what it takes to live the life you were destined to live. You will discover a new vision and create an action plan to transform your life. You will come alive in a new way and be excited to wake up every day.

CHAPTER 1

L = LARGER
Larger vision of yourself beyond your circumstances

"A vision is not just a picture of what could be; it is an appeal to our better selves, a call to become something more."

*~ **Rosabeth Moss Kanter***

I want to share this story about the night I slayed my enemy in a church parking lot; it was then that I learned to live by *The LORI Factor*.

The darkness of that night was blinding. I sat in my car in a church parking lot with tears streaming down my face as I pounded the steering wheel. Bursting out of my car, I began walking down the sidewalk in a rage until I came to a liquor store. *How can I numb this intense pain?* Forcing a smile and hiding my tears, I grabbed a big bottle of liquor and swiftly paid for it.

The warm summer breeze and the smell of evergreen trees would've been a delight on any other night; instead, there was a cold chill inside my mind and body. Brown bag in hand, I walked back to my car, oblivious of my surroundings. Sitting in the driver's seat of my parked car, I unscrewed the bottle of alcohol and poured it into me with the hope of numbing the pain. The enemy then consumed me and took control.

I was going nowhere; just sitting in my parked car. The only thing that was driving then, was alcohol. I plopped out of my car and fell onto some stones. I crawled until I passed out drunk under a truck in that church parking lot.

Prior to that night, I believed I would have brought love and light to others when I signed up for the ministry training class at that church, across the street from my own. Instead, darkness overshadowed me and opened doors from my past, doors I thought were closed. Each week the instructor covered topics including death, divorce, abusive relationships, alcohol abuse, addictions, domestic violence, dysfunctional families, sexual assaults, unhappy women who had abortions, people with abandonment issues, and suchlike.

Each week, I sat on hard metal chairs in the dingy basement classroom of the church. I listened to the instructor present different scenarios and how best to respond to them biblically and with care.

What happened to me that night was the culmination of what the instructor brought out, and things that had been buried inside of me for years. I was at the training class to learn how to minister to others, how to be compassionate, actively listen, and help others cope and heal. Instead, my own experiences were triggered. It was difficult to focus during class, as my past awakened within me. I had experienced some of the situations that were discussed, firsthand; or witnessed loved ones go through them.

One night I looked out of the tiny basement window and saw a rainstorm brewing. It was a sign to warn me of the storm I was about to encounter: the storm brewing in my mind, which would be worse than that impending storm.

I had a beautiful, loving home with a good husband and two wonderful sons. I loved my family. I was living the life I wanted. Unexpectedly, the darkness of my past crept in and devoured my happy home. Apparently, I wasn't aware that I had suppressed hurtful memories and experiences, that then exploded, and left a trail of destruction.

The instructor agreed to help me sort through my triggered memories after class. I thought things were progressing very well. He listened intently and seemed to understand me. I was filled with joy and hope as he took time to guide me through these challenges. The tide turned one night in class (with the whole group present) when my emotions surfaced.

Silent tears were gushing out of me. I did my best to be discreet as I listened to his teaching. The folding chairs were in a half circle. The person next to me whispered, *"Are you okay?"* My classmates signaled to the instructor to address my struggle. They were appalled that he ignored me and just let me cry while he continued to teach.

Finally, he excused himself and escorted me into another room like a naughty child. He told me he would deal with me later, and said I was not allowed back in class ever again. The weight and humiliation of being banished broke me into a million pieces. I bolted from the 'naughty' room into the basement and took to the streets searching for a way to numb my pain. That was the path that led me to that liquor store.

I couldn't take it anymore. The hurt was so intense. He had promised to be there and now I was banned and thrown away like garbage. That is when the landslide occurred. That is how I ended up a broken, intoxicated mess; passed out drunk, under his truck in that church parking lot on that ominous night.

The next thing I knew, I was waking up in an ambulance with my family looking on with concern. The pain on their faces was excruciating. I wasn't capable of pulling myself together; I wasn't okay. I wanted to erase that night. My pain spilled unto those that I love the most.

What had I done?

That night had a domino effect on my life. I was never the same. My new-found drinking habit became out of control almost suddenly, and I slipped into a different world. Pouring the warm liquor into me felt more comforting than the memories of my past. I was constantly confronted by the mistakes I'd made or the things I had seen growing up. Adding to the past, I now had the new memory of being humiliated by the class instructor. My behavior at home was different. I hadn't told my family that I began drinking, but they knew something was definitely wrong.

The shame ate me up and engaging in toxic relationships became my norm. I contemplated ending my life. One day, the suicidal thoughts were so vivid, with all the details of how to end my life; it was convincing. Thankfully, after acting on the plans, I came to myself. That scared me, and my family. That day, I resolved that I was going to do whatever it took to stay alive and be present for my sons.

Well, it's a new day and I have learned to heal from the pain and not bury it. I have learned to forgive myself, and the people who have hurt me. I now love and value myself. I realize that life is God's gift to us, and how we live our lives is our gift to God. *That Lori,* who was under a truck drunk in a church parking lot, is gone. She is dead!

I have embarked on a journey of rebirth; discovering and developing myself to become the best version of me. This transformation resulted in extraordinary gifts emerging through faith, awareness, and belief. No longer am I under that dark spell that had me sleepwalking through life.

What lifestyle do you want? What legacy will you leave? When my earthly assignment is complete, I picture myself with a pen and paper in my hands as I float in a boat on the sea, finishing my race and touching God's face. Every experience we go through is all part of our journey and preparation. I wanted to give up so many times… but God guided me back and He never gave up on me.

I love this quote by Les Brown, *"When life knocks you down, try to land on your back. Because if you can look up, you can get up."* I thank God that I literally landed on my back in life. Because I could look up, I got up and am living life the Lori way. I call it **The LORI Factor**.

Slay the enemy. Create the life of your dreams. Claim your victory. I know you can do it!

You have goals and dreams you want to achieve, right? Have you had moments where you look back on your life and you ask yourself the question, *"What state of mind was I in when I did that?"* Or felt that you were literally out of your mind? You know I was, after reading my dark experience. That incident was a defining moment for me. A defining moment is a moment where you look at yourself and say, *that's not me.*

This Lori that I am now, coupled with my experiences, can take you to the next level. I achieved a larger vision of myself and let go of my limitations and self-destructive behavior; you can too.

LOVE - *What's Love Got to Do with It?*

"Never allow someone to be your priority, while allowing yourself to be their option."

~Unknown

Remember the Tina Turner song that said, *"Oh-oh, what's love got to do, got to do with it? What's love but a second-hand emotion? What's love got to do, got to do with it? Who needs a heart when a heart can be broken?"*

Those broken hearts take time to mend, don't they?

When he walked into the room, the song, *My Girl* by The Temptations was playing. I was captivated by his smile. His voice was a melody that sang to me. I loved when he held me in his arms and danced with me; our steps were in sync. He knew all the right things to say to capture my heart. I believed I was *his* girl, his *only* girl. I guess it was just my imagination running away with me.

Sadly, that turned out to be a toxic relationship. After fifteen years, I finally decided to love myself enough to let go. I realized we were dying together, not growing together. It was hard; my heart hurt deeply. I loved him and part of me always will.

We all want to be loved and accepted. Without love, what's the point? Experiencing real love from the One who loved us first makes all the difference. *That* love is not an illusion: God's love. God loves you, and there is nothing that you can do to make Him stop loving you. That is Good News!

I am aware that many people have different beliefs and different "gods", but my assignment is to be bold enough to speak and write this urgent message. I have been chosen to deliver these truths. All I ask is that you be open to receive and seek the Truth for yourself. My experiences led me down a road of deception that disguised itself as Truth; but I am thankful that I found the right path. Don't shoot the messenger. Thanks for being open minded.

Some may think this part is too *religious*. Really? What does that actually mean? If you read my first book there is a chapter entitled, *Run from Religion*. The word religion is a system of beliefs and rituals, which can create division instead of unity. I am talking about relationships not religion.

Here is an excerpt from my previous book that is worth repeating: *"Hear me out... what matters is Truth and relationship. When I let go of my relationship with my heavenly Father, I literally almost died. Guess what? Hell is a real place. I'm only telling you this because it's a matter of life and death. I almost did not live to give you this message. You can decide whether to accept it or reject it. The universe doesn't have the capacity to love, only God does. He first loved you and created you so that he can have an intimate relationship with you. Ask God for a revelation of His love. Feel the difference. Ask Him to reveal the Truth and show you the way."*

There are different types of love. These four Greek words, Eros, Storge, Philia, and Agape are characterized as romantic love, family love, brotherly love, and God's divine love, which is unconditional and everlasting. Love is not a feeling or emotion, it's a choice. It starts with you.

Do you feel unlovable? Do you wonder why relationships with others do not work? It may be that you never learned to love yourself in a healthy way. Maybe you felt unworthy and had a poor self-image. Self- love is not a selfish or conceited kind of love. It's essential. Know that you have worth, and you will never be worth less; you are worth more than you realize.

Have you chosen to love and accept yourself? The Bible says in 1 John 4:18, *"There is no fear in love, but perfect love casts out fear. For fear has to do with punishment, and whoever fears has not been perfected in love. We love because He first loved us."*

God is love. He created you and loves you more than anyone else could. One undisputed fact is that you need God. We all need God.

When you look into a mirror, do you love the person looking back at you and smile, or do you stick your tongue out with disgust? I admit I did the latter until I learned to value and take better care of myself. Self-care is important; to look and feel good about yourself. Start from within. When you learn how to love yourself, you will attract healthy, right relationships, including the relationship with yourself.

In the kitchen, I placed the bowl on the counter, filled it with ingredients for making cookies, and beat it up. Eating that too often was in reality beating myself up. I ran to the taste and comfort that filled that bowl when I felt empty in my soul. Food was my love language. Milk and cookies had awaited me after school most days when I was growing up. Yet, hearing the words, *"Lori Jane, stop eating those sweets; you'll get fat,"* felt like a setup. However, I continued that habit, and even brought my kids on board with that habit. *Lord, have mercy!*

For too long, I had been poisoning and punishing myself with food, wrong thoughts, and wrong relationships. I had chosen comfort over health. I knew what I needed to do, but I still didn't do it. Why? It took deep reflection. What I discovered was that I believed I didn't deserve better. Words have power. The words I was speaking over myself tore me down. When I turned to God's living word and believed those words, it breathed life and love into me. That's when my heart began to heal. *He heals the brokenhearted and binds up their wounds. Psalm 147:3*

I experienced an epiphany. I realized I couldn't change myself; only God could change me. The way I saw and treated myself wasn't how God saw me. When I looked at myself through God's loving eyes, it was a beautiful picture, which opened the pathway for loving myself, and taking better care of myself. I was finally willing to do my part. Even though I fell back often, I got back up every time.

Accept where you are: be gentle and kind to yourself. Now, let's get your LOVE on. You are clothed with Agape love. It looks good on you.

In 1 Corinthians 13:13 it says, of *"Faith, hope, and love; the greatest of these is love."* Let all you do be done in genuine love. Love is the best motivation that can shift all areas of your life.

Love is the greatest adventure and most valuable treasure of all.

"Greater is He who is in me than he that is in the world." 1 John 4:4.

How you see yourself and how you see others matter. Look through the eyes of the Master. Hear me as I tell you: you are a masterpiece, because you are a piece of the Master.

LEVERAGE - *A Favor to Your Success*

"Service to others leads to greatness."

~ Jim Rohn

"How do you eat an elephant?" Most people say… one bite at a time. A better answer may be… ask for help. Leverage allows you to expand your resources beyond your own limitations. It takes your efforts and multiplies your results; because you get to partner with the resources of others and serve one another. Leverage is utilizing your network and resources to optimize your success. Relationships, partnerships, sponsors, and influencers can create more value and visibility that is mutually beneficial.

What resources and assets do you have? What do you need to achieve your goals and dreams? Be cognizant of what you have to offer. Make a list of people who will consider collaborating with you and brainstorm together. Zig Ziglar said, *"You can have everything in life you want if you will just help other people get what they want."*

The Parable of the Talents, found in the Bible, is relevant here, because when we pool our talents/resources together, it can reap favorable results. If you keep to yourself, don't use your talents, and keep them hidden, you won't benefit from this leverage opportunity.

The proverb, "you reap what you sow," means that future consequences are inevitably shaped by present actions. If you want more love, give more love. If you want encouragement, give encouragement. If you want greater success, help others achieve more. Use your talents, don't deny them or leave them buried.

Maybe you have heard of the parable of the talents in Matthew 25:14-30 MSG, which demonstrates how we utilize or hide our talents:

It's like a man going off on an extended trip. He called his servants together and delegated responsibilities. To one he gave five thousand dollars, to another two thousand, to a third one thousand, depending on their abilities. Then he left. Right off, the first servant went to work and doubled his master's investment. The second did the same. But the man with the single thousand dug a hole and carefully buried his master's money.

After a long absence, the master of those three servants came back and settled up with them. The one given five thousand dollars showed him how he had doubled his investment. His master commended him: 'Good work! You did your job well. From now on, be my partner.'

The servant with the two thousand showed how he also had doubled his master's investment. His master commended him: 'Good work! You did your job well. From now on, be my partner.'

The servant given one thousand said, 'Master, I know you have high standards and hate careless ways, that you demand the best and make no allowances for error. I was afraid I might disappoint you, so I found a good hiding place and secured your money. Here it is, safe and sound down to the last cent.'

The master was furious. 'That's a terrible way to live! It's criminal to live cautiously like that! If you knew I was after the best, why did you do less than the least? The least you could have done would have been to invest the sum with the bankers, where at least I would have gotten a little interest.

'Take the thousand and give it to the one who risked the most. And get rid of this "play-it-safe" who won't go out on a limb. Throw him out into utter darkness.'

Practice sowing, so that you can reap: Use your talents. Build mutually empowering relationships. Remember, honor and gratitude go a long way.

Be aware of the fact that not all people have your best interest at heart. Surround yourself with only quality, influential people. Let me tell you about these people of influence who taught me how to leverage, network, and create connections that are valuable to everyone involved.

I met a man who taught me how to serve my way to success; one who leads by example and from the heart. Many thanks go out to Manny Lopez. As a part of his network, I got connected to influential people and opportunities that I never imagined.

Another person who was influential in my life was my dad. He was an entrepreneur and investor. I must have gotten the entrepreneurial spirit from him. He knew how to collaborate and leverage his network and resources for profitable results.

The right people and connections are out there for me and for you.

We need each other. We are not meant to do/go through life alone.

LIFESTYLE - *Start Living Life on Your Terms*

"Life is short and unpredictable. Eat the dessert first!"

-Helen Keller

Next, I want to talk about visualization and its meaning. Visualization is a powerful tool that can help motivate you to achieve any goal, such as writing a book, making more money, paying off your debts, becoming financially independent, or taking that dream vacation. When you visualize, you focus on something specific — an event, a person, or goal you want to achieve, and picture it in your mind. The outcome you imagine can become your reality. Visualizing creates a path from your current life to your ideal lifestyle.

As you visualize, where are you seeing yourself in life? Is it on the beach with your toes in the sand? Is it skiing on a mountain? Is it flying your airplane? Is it eating s'mores around the campfire with your family? Is it dancing cheek to cheek with your sweetie (or with your teddy bear if you don't have a sweetie)?

There are so many scenarios. Close your eyes and picture the life you desire first in your mind. See it, hear it, taste it, smell it, feel it. Where do you want to live? Who do you want to hang out with? How much money do you want to make? What do you love?

Get a clear vision and think about why it's important and keep it in the forefront of your mind. Make it tangible; write it down. For example, some people like to create a vision board. Picture it daily and soon it will become your reality as you take action steps toward realizing it. Surround yourself with the type of people and places that bring joy and fit into your vision. Test drive the car you want to own. Talk to people who are where you want to be.

Speaking of cars, the car I had was worn out, and for months I didn't drive, because it wasn't safe to drive it. I got rid of it. I pictured a better, safer car in my driveway, paid in full. I didn't know how or when it would happen, but the first step was believing and visualizing it. I prayed that God would make a way, and He did.

One day, my son and daughter-in-love (yes, I said love) called me outside and handed me keys to a car they bought for me. That was my miracle car. It became reality. I am thankful.

Kayaking is therapeutic and enjoyable for me. My kayak had a hole in it. I longingly watched everyone else kayaking on the water. I didn't have the budget at the time to get it fixed or buy a new one. Despite those circumstances, I prayed and visualized myself kayaking on the water again. One day, someone asked if they could store their kayaks in my garage and said I could use them as well. Now, I am on the water again, which is a pleasure that I truly treasure. Believe it's possible and put a high value on the lifestyle you were born to live.

I knew the way I was living was not meant for me. There is so much more to do and for me to see. I love the sea. I see myself paddling in a kayak, which I have done many times, but my bigger vision is cruising on a yacht with a private chef, having fun with family and friends, and the sun shining on the water. The rhythm rocks us gently as the yacht glides across the sea. What's your vision?

Joyce Meyer says, *"I may not be where I want to be but thank God I am not where I used to be."*

Think about a sculptor who starts with a shapeless, undefined object. Taking the hammer and chisel in hand, the artist removes what he doesn't need. The pieces are chipped away that don't belong to let his vision emerge and come alive. Knowing what you don't want can also help you figure out what you do want.

Commit to your dreams and take just one step at a time consistently. Stay in action and revise and tweak as you go along. Just don't give up; don't stop. Keep reading, there's more...

LEGACY - *Live a Life That Outlives You*

"The wealthiest places in the world are not gold mines, oil fields, diamond mines or banks. The wealthiest place is the cemetery. There lies companies that were never started, masterpieces that were never painted... In the cemetery there is buried the greatest treasure of untapped potential. There is a treasure within you that must come out. Don't go to the grave with your treasure still within YOU."

~ Dr. Myles Munroe

What if you died today? Would you be remembered? Did you use your gifts and talents to make a difference and leave a legacy? If you haven't yet, it's not too late.

You have something special. Maybe you haven't recognized it or have figured it out yet. If you dig deep enough, you will discover talents you never knew you had. Start by identifying any limiting beliefs and behaviors that are not the real you. Keep in mind that you need to have a larger vision of yourself beyond where you are now. Write letters to your future self. Visualize the best version of you and hold that picture in your mind and heart.

Purpose in your heart to make a difference. After discovering your gifts and talents, use them to create timeless gifts and live a life that outlives you. My daughter-in-love, Stefanie, resisted her artistic talents for years. Then, she was able to remove her blocks and beliefs that her art wasn't good enough or that she wouldn't have enough paint and supplies. Her art is amazing! She is amazing! Once she changed her environment and let God flow through her, prophetic drawings, paintings, and photos emerged. Using her talents continues to bless many.

Years ago, I wrote and framed poems I gave to the teachers who taught my sons. Recently, one teacher said the poem I wrote is still hanging up in her home. That is a timeless gift that keeps on giving.

You may have heard that it's important to know your "why". My "why" and my legacy are my sons and their wives as well as the books I write and speeches I share. My "why" is also you: helping you uncover the greatness within you and helping to bring it out of you.

Speaking of sons, both of mine are precious gifts. Joseph is a man of God who has stepped into his greatness. He uses his talents in many ways, especially in business. His heart to help people and step out in faith continues to make a difference in many lives, especially mine. His keen ear for listening and understanding is a gift. Kevin has a talent for mechanics and loves to tinker. He is the chief of a local fire department and that speaks for itself. First responders are essential. Both my sons are hardworking men. They are precious gifts to me. As for me, writing is one talent and passion. What are your gifts and talents?

Here is a result of using my writing talent. A dear soul wrote a review thanking me and telling me how what I wrote impacted her life. That makes it all worth it. I know it's not about me, it's what I was put here to do for others.

The book review started like this… *"After a very long and hard day I filled a tub with hot water & Epsom salts and finally grabbed this book I had been meaning to read for months. Well, I had to keep adding hot water to my tub over the next 2 plus hours because I couldn't put the book down. An easy read you won't want to put down."*

What legacy will you leave? Your legacy is a timeless treasure.

There is a special place in life,
A goal I must attain,

A dream that I must follow,
For I won't be back again.

There is a mark that I must leave,
However small it be,

A Legacy of love for those,
Who follow after me.

~ ***Grace E. Easley***

CHAPTER 2

O = OPTIMISM

A favorable outlook and belief you can change your life

> *"Optimism is the faith that leads to achievement. Nothing can be done without faith and confidence."*
>
> *~ Helen Keller*

Optimism is more than just positive thinking; there is a difference. It is important to clarify the differences. Optimism is having hope and confidence for a successful outcome. It is more than just thinking positive thoughts and saying affirmations. Affirmations can cause you to feel like you are lying to yourself if your belief isn't there yet. How do you know when you believe it though? When you feel it. You have to feel it!

Having an optimistic spirit is a game changer. The reason I engaged in that negative, self-destructive behavior before was because I had a limited vision of myself. When you achieve a larger vision of yourself, beyond the negative people that you used to hang around with, and beyond the negative choices that have brought you to that place of ruin, you will see yourself from a different perspective.

I developed an optimistic spirit by choosing to work on myself, cultivating a different kind of way in which to view myself. I encourage you to do that as well. Develop a larger vision of yourself by doing more, achieving more, and moving beyond the negative habits and behaviors that have kept you stuck.

Be optimistic! Say, *"Hey, I can do this. I can make this change in my life."* Become like Mother Theresa who said, *"We are all pencils in the hand of God writing love letters to the world."* As you discover your talents and envision your future life, start writing a new chapter in your life and give the pencil to God. God is still writing your story, quit trying to steal the pencil. Trust the Author.

OVERCOMER - *Bust Through Obstacles*

"Success is to be measured not so much by the position that one has reached in life as by the obstacles he has overcome."

~ Booker T. Washington

I want you to think about defining moments in your life. How did those moments mold you into who you are today?

There was music playing in the restaurant where I took my lunch break. I enjoyed the break from the stressful temporary job assignment. Suddenly, a tingling sensation came over the right side of my face. A wave of dizziness hit me, and it sounded like a concert was playing in my ear. I love to dance, but this wasn't the time to bust a move.

Quickly exiting the eating place, I made it to my car, but I felt worse. After calling the agency to inform them that I could not return to work, I drove myself to the emergency room. I wondered if I was having a stroke. Eventually, I was brought in and had testing done. Thankfully, the doctors ruled out a stroke. They were not exactly sure what was wrong. I was told to follow up with my primary doctor and was released.

I was devastated when I woke up the next morning and looked in the mirror. My face was disfigured and droopy; my speech was slurred, and I had lost my smile. Tears welled up, but no tears came out of my right eye; it was dry. I was not able to close my right eye and had to tape it shut at night. What had hit me? Bell's Palsy!

I know my Creator has me on the potter's wheel and keeps molding me like clay, but seriously? Did it have to be literally? Have mercy! That was a defining and devastating moment. It was hard to face my own face.

As I write this, it is not yet completely recovered, but it has come a long way.

Oh yes, there were challenges. What challenges have you faced and have overcome? What did you discover about yourself in the process? Pearl Bailey said, *"You never find yourself until you face the truth."*

No matter what I looked like, no matter my circumstances, my truth was realizing that it was time to get onto platforms for my voice and message to be heard. **I am a messenger of HOPE** to give you hope for the future and **POWER** in the present. We all have a higher purpose. Do you know that you have more inside you that's waiting to come out?

In digging and searching, what did you find? What are the desires of your heart? What are you HUNGERING to do? Write a book, speak, sing a song, paint, invent, create, coach, teach, start a business? **God doesn't call the qualified, He qualifies the called.**

Write this down: **I declare I will reach my highest potential.**

Now, with the help of God, turn your situation around and fight for your dreams. Expect things to get better. I went through a physical transfiguration of my face, but I also continue on the transformation path in every other area of my life. You can grow and transform as well. There is so much more for you; just celebrate what you have already overcome. **Make a list and congratulate yourself on coming this far.**

What are your current thoughts and challenges? Look at where you may be overthinking or overreacting, for these can cause you to become overwhelmed. Overwhelmed is not knowing what to do next. Take a deep breath and keep going at your own pace. Every thought you act on will give you a result. When you think a new thought, you get a new result.

Think about Jesus; give Him a chance. Ultimately, Jesus gives us the assurance that He has given us the power to overcome all the power of the enemy, and nothing shall harm us. How do I know? When I let go of

Him, I almost died due to self-destructive behavior, destructive thoughts, and wrong actions.

We've all had different types of interruptions in our lives. There will always be interruptions in life; but don't focus on those things because you will become paralyzed with fear.

*"When the end comes for you, let it find you conquering a new mountain, not sliding down an old one. Your life, my life is either a warning or an example; a warning of what not to do or an example of what to do." - **Jim Rohn***

Instead of thinking of things as interruptions, think of them as interludes. Allow the interlude to give you space to pause and reflect on the moment; change direction if needed and do what you need to do.

We were enjoying lunch on the deck: the pastor, his wife, and I. The pastor had recently preached a sermon about turning interruptions into interludes. My sons and the neighbor girl were riding their bikes. During our conversation, one of my sons approached me saying that the girl fell off her bike and was hurt. I excused myself to get the girl while my son filled in entertaining our guests. When I returned and took a deep breath, I asked, *"Was that what you call an interlude?"* The pastor smiled and replied, *"You were listening."*

Listen, learn, and be flexible. Sometimes we need to pause and be still or change direction. Interludes may lead to a new path. Stay calm and enjoy the adventure always. Having a sense of humor helps too.

OPEN - *Keep Your Heart and Mind Open to the Truth*

Jesus said, *"I am the way, the truth, and the life. No one comes to the Father except through me."*

- John 14:6

Open your heart and mind but only to the Truth. No matter what you believe… ask and seek the only true God, He will show and reveal the Truth to you. When I found God, I found true love. I introduce you to my God. The One who transformed my life. The God of mercy. The God of love.

The speaker at a meeting was telling her story. In closing, she gave God the Glory. Ugh! I sat in the audience with my arms crossed, rolling my eyes. Not that 'God stuff' again. I thought I was here to learn about business.

What I didn't know then is that putting God as CEO in your business was essential. My mind was closed. I wasn't able to hear and receive what anyone was saying. I do remember being intrigued by a particular book on the table that I had bought: **"See You at the Top,"** by Zig Ziglar.

I still have that book and it's time to read it again. A big part of my entrepreneurial journey began at that meeting. It was a Divine appointment, but I didn't know it at that time. From then until now, I have become more open and willing to listen, learn, grow and be coachable. Believing and receiving my Higher Power, and opening my heart and mind to God surely put me on the right path and saved my life. I am glad He didn't give up on me.

Him, I almost died due to self-destructive behavior, destructive thoughts, and wrong actions.

We've all had different types of interruptions in our lives. There will always be interruptions in life; but don't focus on those things because you will become paralyzed with fear.

*"When the end comes for you, let it find you conquering a new mountain, not sliding down an old one. Your life, my life is either a warning or an example; a warning of what not to do or an example of what to do." - **Jim Rohn***

Instead of thinking of things as interruptions, think of them as interludes. Allow the interlude to give you space to pause and reflect on the moment; change direction if needed and do what you need to do.

We were enjoying lunch on the deck: the pastor, his wife, and I. The pastor had recently preached a sermon about turning interruptions into interludes. My sons and the neighbor girl were riding their bikes. During our conversation, one of my sons approached me saying that the girl fell off her bike and was hurt. I excused myself to get the girl while my son filled in entertaining our guests. When I returned and took a deep breath, I asked, *"Was that what you call an interlude?"* The pastor smiled and replied, *"You were listening."*

Listen, learn, and be flexible. Sometimes we need to pause and be still or change direction. Interludes may lead to a new path. Stay calm and enjoy the adventure always. Having a sense of humor helps too.

OPEN - *Keep Your Heart and Mind Open to the Truth*

Jesus said, *"I am the way, the truth, and the life. No one comes to the Father except through me."*

- John 14:6

Open your heart and mind but only to the Truth. No matter what you believe… ask and seek the only true God, He will show and reveal the Truth to you. When I found God, I found true love. I introduce you to my God. The One who transformed my life. The God of mercy. The God of love.

The speaker at a meeting was telling her story. In closing, she gave God the Glory. Ugh! I sat in the audience with my arms crossed, rolling my eyes. Not that 'God stuff' again. I thought I was here to learn about business.

What I didn't know then is that putting God as CEO in your business was essential. My mind was closed. I wasn't able to hear and receive what anyone was saying. I do remember being intrigued by a particular book on the table that I had bought: **"See You at the Top,"** by Zig Ziglar.

I still have that book and it's time to read it again. A big part of my entrepreneurial journey began at that meeting. It was a Divine appointment, but I didn't know it at that time. From then until now, I have become more open and willing to listen, learn, grow and be coachable. Believing and receiving my Higher Power, and opening my heart and mind to God surely put me on the right path and saved my life. I am glad He didn't give up on me.

Open-mindedness will help you to learn and grow, strengthening your belief in yourself. Only God is all knowing. If you have the mind of Christ He will direct your ways. Be led by the Holy Spirit (not by other spirits that can be deceptive and cause harm). The Bible is not a book of rules. It reveals God's heart, a Father's heart full of love and compassion. He created you. He created the universe.

As the messenger, this is what I feel led to tell you. This world has many religions, diverse beliefs, and cultures. Think about it: being born of a virgin had only happened when Mary gave birth to Jesus.

What makes Jesus different? First, let's revisit the word "religion," which is actually division. Religion is human efforts to get to God. Jesus is God coming in the flesh to us. No comparison. Did you know Jesus' mission was to get rid of religion? Religion is bondage with rules. True freedom, love and life is found in the Savior who died for you. Ask Him yourself. Again, I would be remiss if I didn't tell you. Ultimately, you need to seek the Truth yourself.

Jesus gives you eternal life. Kingdom authority allows His power to flow through you. Just so you know the difference, the Bible is the Law of Attraction book. Another book, which will remain a *secret*, has good points but focuses on self and leaves out Jesus. Receive His grace and mercy by opening the greatest Book of all- the Bible. Heaven is our Homeland Security. When you awaken to God's love, you're empowered with His life. Beloved, you are adored, cherished, and treasured.

Don't get it twisted. A half-truth is a whole lie. Don't let the enemy and the voice of religion or spirituality fool you. There are many counterfeits. Spirituality can mean many things and are often rooted in realms that open dangerous doors.

How do I know? I was deceived and almost died because of many "spiritual" things that sounded and looked like God. We can't earn our way into heaven doing good works. It's not about logic or light. *"... for even Satan disguises himself as an angel of light."* -2 Corinthians 11:14.

Hear the voice of God. There is no other love like His. Our beliefs filter what we see. *"Do not turn to mediums or necromancers; do not seek them out, and so make yourselves unclean by them: I am the Lord your God."- Leviticus 19:31*

Do you know where you're going when you die? No joke. It's a good thing I didn't die when I let go of God, because I didn't feel worthy and didn't think even He could love me. That's when I turned to alcohol and wanted to die. Satan comes to kill, steal, and destroy. At that time, I would have been on my way to hell. Yes, it's a real place.

I am thankful God didn't give up on me even when I gave up on myself. This decision is imperative. It's literally a matter of life and death. I know how the story ends and where I will be when I leave this earthly body. I am thankful for second chances.

Some people don't believe in anything, and some are being deceived. I know, for I was deceived at one time. I am thankful I had another chance to know the Truth. No matter what you believe, give me a listening ear. I know my life was saved so that I could relay this message to you. That's my mission. The choice is yours, of course, whether to receive this message or not. If your god is not the True God, it/he can't work for you. I introduce to you my God, the True God. Try Him and see what happens. Trust me, you will not be disappointed. What He did for me, He'll do for you.

Many people turn to outside things to feel fulfilled: Drugs, alcohol, sex, cults, worshipping the moon, sun, or other idols, just to name a few. They are blinded by pain, ignorance, other gods, idols, pride, and don't have ears to hear or eyes to see beyond the pain and deception. I was there too to some degree. I'm glad the Lord, the True God, delivered me.

I wasn't an unbeliever per se, who refused to believe or accept the Truth. It all depends on how we were taught, and how we understood what we were taught. From my experience, I can see how people choose different paths, because we all have free wills.

I asked for God to help my unbelief and doubt. I learned that unbelief is saying that we don't believe Jesus, the Son of God was the final sacrifice to take away our sins and give us eternal life. That wasn't it, I did believe that. Natural unbelief is when we are moved by what we see, so if we can't see it, we don't believe it. I had faith in what was unseen.

There was a disconnect with the religious teaching that I learned, which was based on performance, rules, and rituals instead of what Jesus did. When we endeavor to make ourselves right with God based on our own efforts, it can't work. When I was open to receive His love, grace, and mercy, a powerful connection was created.

You must open your heart to God to receive healing and learn to forgive. You must forgive yourself and others, and be honest. Forgiveness is crucial for your own healing. What blocked me and kept me stuck was a spirit of unforgiveness. I was not willing to forgive.

It was dark. Loud music was playing and everyone had paper and pen in hand. The event leader directed us to write down the names of those who we needed to forgive. It was then I realized that at the top of my list was ME. I broke down in tears, but it was a breakthrough moment for ME. It was then that I realized why the music was playing loudly. It was so that the cries of many could not be heard, as everyone was being exposed to himself/herself.

Like an onion that has many layers, so we have many layers of healing; peeling them away one by one. It's a process. That revelation set me on a healing path. Each layer peeled away has lifted me to new levels each day.

Unwillingness to forgive fills us with resentment, which produces a root of bitterness that poisons our entire system. Bitterness is a form of bondage. Bondage is when we are under control or influenced by someone or something. It's like slavery. Things happen in our lives: we get hurt, our hearts get broken, we have deep regrets. Those things are like having a pair of handcuffs around our hearts' wrists, and they hinder us from fulfilling our God-given dreams and passions.

Forgiveness releases bitter bondage. An unforgiving nature can manifest into physical pain, sickness, and disease. Like the song in the movie Frozen says, *"Let It Go."*

Opening your mind and heart will reveal the obstacles, blocks, and limiting beliefs that have kept you stuck, and feeling hopeless, unworthy, angry, lonely, depressed, and defeated. Rewrite those stories and see yourself in victory.

"Never let someone's opinion become your reality. Never sacrifice who you are because someone else has a problem with it. Love who you are inside and out." -Les Brown.

OBEDIENCE - *An Act of Faith*

"Obedience to God is the pathway to the life you really want to live."

~ Joyce Meyer

Obedience is respecting and trusting with faith. God has made incredible promises and has linked them to our obedience. It's the "if and then" promises of the Living Word. If we obey what He says, then He promises that He'll save us, watch over us, take care of us and supply our needs. On the flipside, disobedience has unfavorable consequences. It's okay; we are all human. Forgive yourself and keep it movin'.

I used to resist the word 'obedience,' not knowing who the True God was. I am thankful that I am no longer on a destructive, lost path. I now know who I am and *Whose* I am.

Here is what I know from the Truth of God's Word in Jeremiah 29:11-13. *"For I know the plans I have for you,"* declares the Lord, *"plans to give you hope and a future. Then you will call on me and come and pray to me, and I will listen to you. You will seek me and find me when you seek me with all your heart."*

We are all here on God's appointment for a purpose. You are never alone when you surrender to God. Call on Him and He will hear you. He is never too busy. He keeps His promises and cannot lie. Experience His love and compassion for you, if you haven't already done so.

I have learned that surrender is better than rebellion and resistance. I had my season of rebellion. Since I can't cancel the consequences or go back in time, I keep the hard lessons I have learned. It's all part of the journey.

The fruit of obedience gives the freedom to progress and be who we really ought to be through obeying God, our Creator, the divine Principle of the universe. Rebellion, resistance, and obstacles get in our way and cause blockages. Some common blockers are fear, guilt, anger, self-sabotage, envy, and lack of focus. I remember learning that anger turned inward leads to depression.

If you have experienced any of those blockers, don't beat yourself up. It's all part of the journey of life. There are ways to remove those blockers. I can guide you through a process of how to do that if you will allow me. Everyone has his/her difficult moments. The key is not to stay stuck in those moments. Keep overcoming by the power of God. Stay optimistic

OPPORTUNITIES - *Right Opportunities Change Lives*

"A mentor is someone who sees more talent and ability within you, than you see in yourself, and helps bring it out of you."

~ Bob Proctor

Instead of looking back, choose to focus on what you want and where you're going.

Here's what I have discovered: It's important to have mentors who speak life into you with love without beating you down. You may feel unworthy and undeserving to have mentors of high value. Maybe you think the only way to reach mentors of that level requires you to be wealthy. The rich get richer, right?

No matter how many times you have fought to raise your revenue, it still wasn't enough, and you thought **you** weren't enough. So, you gave up and settled for surviving instead of thriving. But that **HUNGER** was still stirring; it kept rising up. You did what you could on your own, but you kept running into obstacles. You overcame some, but you couldn't do it **all** on your own. Another defining moment occurred when the right people came into your life. It takes a team; a dream team who will help you live your dreams.

I was at an event, sitting in the back. I noticed a young, dark, handsome man standing there. I got up the courage to introduce myself. I said, *"Hi, I'm Lori. I am new here and feel a little out of the loop."* With his kind smile, he put his arm around me and said, *"You're not out of the loop anymore. You are family now."* I didn't catch his name the first time, so I asked, *"What's your name again?"* He said, *"John Leslie Brown."*

"You are Les Brown's son?" I asked. *"I have been praying for your dad and family for so long. How is he?"*

Tears welled up in his eyes and he said, *"Thank you. He is doing well."*

He then looked into my eyes and said, *"There is something special about you."* Whoa, that took my breath away. No one had ever said that to me before. That was a divine defining moment that changed my life.

In Romans 8:28 it says, *"We know that in all things God works for the good of those who love him, who have been called according to his purpose."*

As Flavia Weedn says, *"Some people come into our lives and quickly go. Some stay for a while, leave footprints on our hearts, and we are never, ever the same."*

Who has left footprints on your heart? Treasure those moments. People come into your life for a reason, a season, or a lifetime. When God connects people together, that becomes a sure connection, and for certain, it's for a great purpose.

What has happened for you that made you feel special and valued? The best is yet to come. Matthew 22:14 in the Bible says, *"Many are called but few are chosen."* I am chosen, and so are you.

I want to share these key points with you:

- Raise your awareness of who and what are around you.

- Find like-minded people who believe in you and encourage you.

- Network and brainstorm ideas. Set your course.

- Opportunities will find you and you will discover opportunities as long as you keep pursuing them.

- Know it's possible; recognize and seize the right opportunities, and the right people who line up with your values, beliefs, and dreams.

CHAPTER 3

R = REINVENT Yourself

Make A Radical Change in Your Life

"Life isn't about finding yourself. Life is about creating yourself."
*~ **George Bernard Shaw***

The next factor that you will have to consider is to REINVENT yourself. There needs to be a radical change in how you've been showing up in life. There is a reason why Paul said in 1 Corinthians 15:31, *"I die daily."*

Here is a direct message (paraphrase) from Paul, in The Message, to reveal revelation. 1 Corinthians 15: 1-2 *Friends, let me go over the Message with you one final time—this Message that I proclaimed and that you made your own; this Message on which you took your stand and by which your life has been saved. (I'm assuming, now, that your belief was the real thing and not a passing fancy, that you're in this for good and holding fast.)*

3-9 The first thing I did was place before you what was placed so emphatically before me: that the Messiah died for our sins, exactly as Scripture tells it; that He was buried; that He was raised from death on the third day, again exactly as Scripture says; that He presented himself alive to Peter, then to his closest followers, and later to more than five hundred of his followers all at the same time, most of them still around (although a few have since died); that He then spent time with James and the rest of those He commissioned to represent Him; and that He finally presented himself alive to me. It was fitting that I bring up the rear. I don't deserve to be included in that inner circle, as you well know, having spent all those early years trying my best to stamp God's church right out of existence.

10-11 But because God was so gracious, so very generous, here I am. And I'm not about to let His grace go to waste. Haven't I worked hard trying to do more than any of the others? Even then, my work didn't amount to all that much. It was God giving me the work to do, God giving me the energy to do it. So, whether you heard it from me or from those others, it's all the same: We spoke God's truth and you entrusted your lives.

12-15 Now, let me ask you something profound yet troubling. If you became believers because you trusted the proclamation that Christ is alive, risen from the dead, how can you let people say that there is no such thing as a resurrection? If there's no resurrection, there's no living Christ. And face it—if there's no resurrection for Christ, everything we've told you is smoke and mirrors, and everything you've staked your life on is smoke and mirrors. Not only that, but we would be guilty of telling a string of barefaced lies about God, all these affidavits we passed on to you verifying that God raised up Christ—sheer fabrications if there's no resurrection.

16-20 If corpses can't be raised, then Christ wasn't, because he was indeed dead. And if Christ weren't raised, then all you're doing is wandering about in the dark, as lost as ever. It's even worse for those who died hoping in Christ and resurrection, because they're already in their graves. If all we get out of Christ is a little inspiration for a few short years, we're a pretty sorry lot. But the truth is that Christ has been raised up, the first in a long legacy of those who are going to leave the cemeteries.

21-28 *There is a nice symmetry in this: Death initially came by a man, and resurrection from death came by a man. Everybody dies in Adam; everybody comes alive in Christ. But we have to wait our turn: Christ is first, then those with Him at his Coming, the grand consummation when, after crushing the opposition, He hands over his kingdom to God the Father. He won't let up until the last enemy is down—and the very last enemy is death! As the psalmist said, "He laid them low, one and all; He walked all over them." When Scripture says that "He walked all over them," it's obvious that He couldn't at the same time be walked on. When everything and everyone is finally under God's rule, the Son will step down, taking his place with everyone else, showing that God's rule is absolutely comprehensive—a perfect ending!*

29 *Why do you think people offer themselves to be baptized for those already in the grave? If there's no chance of resurrection for a corpse, if God's power stops at the cemetery gates, why do we keep doing things that suggest He's going to clean the place out someday, pulling everyone up on their feet alive?*

30-33 *And why do you think I keep risking my neck in this dangerous work? I look death in the face practically every day I live. Do you think I'd do this if I wasn't convinced of your resurrection and mine as guaranteed by the resurrected Messiah Jesus? Do you think I was just trying to act heroic when I fought the wild beasts at Ephesus, hoping it wouldn't be the end of me? Not on your life! It's resurrection, resurrection, always resurrection, that undergirds what I do and say, the way I live. If there's no resurrection, "We eat, we drink, the next day we die," and that's all there is to it. But don't fool yourselves. Don't let yourselves be poisoned by this anti-resurrection loose talk. "Bad company ruins good manners."*

34 *Think straight. Awaken to the holiness of life. No more playing fast and loose with resurrection facts. Ignorance of God is a luxury you can't afford in times like these. Aren't you embarrassed that you've let this kind of thing go on as long as you have?*

35-38 Some skeptic is sure to ask, "Show me how resurrection works. Give me a diagram; draw me a picture. What does this 'resurrection body' look like?" If you look at this question closely, you realize how absurd it is. There are no diagrams for this kind of thing. We do have a parallel experience in gardening. You plant a "dead" seed; soon there is a flourishing plant. There is no visual likeness between seed and plant. You could never guess what a tomato would look like by looking at a tomato seed. What we plant in the soil and what grows out of it don't look anything alike. The dead body that we bury in the ground and the resurrection body that comes from it will be dramatically different.

39-41 You will notice that the variety of bodies is stunning. Just as there are different kinds of seeds, there are different kinds of bodies—humans, animals, birds, fish—each unprecedented in its form. You get a hint at the diversity of resurrection glory by looking at the diversity of bodies not only on earth but in the skies—sun, moon, stars—all these varieties of beauty and brightness. And we're only looking at pre-resurrection "seeds"—who can imagine what the resurrection "plants" will be like!

42-44 This image of planting a dead seed and raising a live plant is a mere sketch at best, but perhaps it will help in approaching the mystery of the resurrection body—but only if you keep in mind that when we're raised, we're raised for good, alive forever! The corpse that's planted is no beauty, but when it's raised, it's glorious. Put in the ground weak, it comes up powerful. The seed sown is natural; the seed grown is supernatural—same seed, same body, but what a difference from when it goes down in physical mortality to when it is raised up in spiritual immortality!

45-49 We follow this sequence in Scripture: The First Adam received life; the Last Adam is a life-giving Spirit. Physical life comes first, then spiritual—a firm base shaped from the earth, a final completion coming out of heaven. The First Man was made out of earth, and people since then are earthy; the Second Man was made out of heaven, and people now can be heavenly. In the same way that we've worked from our earthy origins, let's embrace our heavenly ends.

50 I need to emphasize, friends, that our natural, earthy lives don't in themselves lead us by their very nature into the kingdom of God. Their very "nature" is to die, so how could they "naturally" end up in the Life kingdom?

51-57 But let me tell you something wonderful, a mystery I'll probably never fully understand. We're not all going to die—but we are all going to be changed. You hear a blast to end all blasts from a trumpet, and in the time that you look up and blink your eyes—it's over. On signal from that trumpet from heaven, the dead will be up and out of their graves, beyond the reach of death, never to die again. At the same moment and in the same way, we'll all be changed. In the resurrection scheme of things, this has to happen: everything perishable taken off the shelves and replaced by the imperishable, this mortal replaced by the immortal. Then the saying will come true:

Death swallowed by triumphant Life! Who got the last word, oh, Death?

Oh, Death, who's afraid of you now?

It was sin that made death so frightening and law-code guilt that gave sin its leverage, its destructive power. But now in a single victorious stroke of Life, all three—sin, guilt, death—are gone, the gift of our Master, Jesus Christ. Thank God!

58 With all this going for us, my dear, dear friends, stand your ground. And don't hold back. Throw yourselves into the work of the Master, confident that nothing you do for him is a waste of time or effort.

Paul was referring to the persecution and risk of sharing the resurrection. I, too, decided to take a risk and share all this with you. I shared that scripture so you can understand that I had to die to self. *That Lori, who was under a truck drunk in a church parking lot, is gone. She's dead!*

I had to reinvent myself and reclaim my life. I had to be willing to carve out the time to work on myself and take responsibility for where I was in life. Tick, Tock, time is short. We all have an expiration date on this planet.

Like I said earlier, forgiving myself was essential. Making changes in how I behaved: what I listened to and watched, and speaking words of life, not death, over myself shifted my direction. Reading the Book of Life, and books written by successful thought leaders, listening to motivational messages, and training my brain, all fed me with determination and inspiration.

The other key component of my reinvention was assessing my relationships. How, and with whom, are you spending your time? Another learning curve for me was understanding and setting boundaries, as well as identifying the toxic relationships in my life. The people you surround yourself with can either be harmful or helpful. It was time to detox and stop drinking the 'Kool-Aid'.

It was time to stop allowing myself to be disrespected and devalued. For example, when I was once in a relationship where he held the door open for other women, but not for me. There are many more examples, but you get the picture, right? It can also be men being treated badly as well. Ladies, treat your man like a king and he will treat you like his queen. If not, it may not be the right match. Go where you're celebrated, not merely tolerated. You deserve more.

This is what I did:

- I started by celebrating myself.

- I took better care of myself.

- I took time to have fun, which helped to relieve stress.

- I took 3 meds daily:

    - 1) Laughter

    - 2) Vitamin T3

    - 3) Vitamin W3

- What are Vitamins T3 and W3 you ask? Vitamin **T3** is writing down at least **3** things I am **thankful** for each day.

- Vitamin **W3** is writing down and celebrating **3 wins** that I accomplished each day.

You can create the life you were designed to live; and get to enjoy it however you please, and with the people you choose.

RISKS - *Success requires Sacrifice*

"There is freedom waiting for you, On the breezes of the sky, And you ask, 'What if I fall?' Oh, but my darling, what if you fly?"

– *Erin Hanson*

Risks are necessary to achieve success. You may have to face the fear and take the risk anyway despite the uncertainty. Risks require courage. Disrupt negative thoughts and emotions. First, acknowledge them, because you can't change what you don't acknowledge. Break out of complacency. Get uncomfortable and go pursue the desires of your heart. Be assertive! Be compelling! Fly high!

Speaking of flying, I boarded an airplane to San Diego, thanks to a generous invitation. It was a risk. It was also an opportunity for adventure because I got to attend an event where I met new people. It was nice to get the invitation from a woman I had recently connected with in a group we had in common. She invited me to stay at her apartment. Unfortunately, the original plans and accommodation fell through many times. I was excited about sunny San Diego, but often I was confined inside, in the dark.

One day, I arranged to venture out. It involved taking different forms of transportation including taxis and trains. On the way back, I waited for the last train, in the dark. Where did all the people go? I was alone with my backpack sitting on a bench. Suddenly, a man appeared with a backpack and asked if I was waiting for the same train. The train never came. There I was in a vulnerable situation with Henry, the Homeless Guy. He thought I was homeless too.

At that point, we agreed to share a taxi. He said he had a hotel reserved and invited me to stay with him. *What? Oh no!* He said he would sleep on the floor. *Yeah, right.* He was more than just homeless since he wanted me alone in a room with him. That would have been a dangerous, compromising situation, and possibly deadly. I know, I know. My mother always said I was naïve and too nice.

After dropping off Henry, the taxi driver delivered me safely back to the apartment that night. A couple days went by and staying at the apartment didn't work out. I had to get out quickly. Finding different accommodations was not in my budget, so someone suggested a low-cost alternative… a hostel.

Talk about an experience! Here I was surrounded by many foreign college students; some didn't speak English. It was cold and cramped. Bunk beds were lined up, and I woke up to someone new almost daily. Did I mention it was co-ed? No privacy, vomit in the shared bathroom sink, probably from someone's hangover, and my belongings could not be secured. It was a booze fest all the time. I needed to wash my clothes and bought pods for soap. They were supposed to dissolve in the washing machine but that didn't happen. The washer wasn't working right and didn't spin out the water. I had to wring out my clothes by hand. Gross, messy, and heavy. Yuck!

I was thankful people weren't hostile in the hostel; they were friendly for the most part. The location was right on the ocean, my favorite place to be, by the sea. I enjoyed writing, walking, and capturing pictures of the surfers and scenery. That was my risky, uncomfortable, but fun adventure overall. *Note to self: Online descriptions can be deceiving.*

When I was sitting by the ocean, I captured amazing pictures of the surfers. I treasure that time, and the people I met; it was worth the risk.

RESPONSIBILITY - *Break Up with Self-Sabotage and Reclaim Your Power*

"The price of greatness is responsibility."

*- **Winston Churchill***

Tragedy happens to us all. You can let it destroy you or you can build upon it. It doesn't matter **what** happened, what matters is, *what are you going to do about it?*

I've done things I am not proud of, which resulted in self-hatred. I let the guilt and shame eat at me for too long. I knew I had hurt people, but the one I was hurting the most was myself. Staying in that place of guilt and shame was robbing me of who I was created to be.

A family member made a suggestion to me, as to how I should deal with a situation that I had gotten myself into. He thought it would ruin my life if I didn't do what he said. I know he was trying to protect me and believed his recommendation was best. However, it turned out that it ruined my life by following his direction. Now I know that it was that suggestion that opened the door to self-hatred, self-sabotage, guilt, and shame. During this period, I felt unloved, unlovable, and empty; and that's when I let go of God. I didn't know that He was the only One, and the only Way to love and to salvation. I had given up. I stopped believing in God; I stopped believing in myself.

It may look like there is no way out for some; and that's the reason why many resort to suicide. The suicide rates are rising rapidly. Many people resort to suicide, not because they want to end their lives, but they just want their pain to end. When they get to that point, they cannot think rationally or see a way out.

Remember: Suicide is a permanent solution to a temporary problem.

I thought suicide was the answer and an end to my pain. I thought I would be in heaven where there are no more tears and no more suffering. I thought I'd stand before God's throne and hear Him say about the life I did live, *"Good and faithful servant, job well done."* But, if I had succeeded in taking my own life, this is what I'd hear, *"You good and faithless servant, job incomplete."*

When you die, it's not the end (if you decide to choose Jesus). It's eternal life with Him. I know I don't want to miss out on my mansion in heaven and eternal life. The best life ever.

I am thankful that I didn't succeed with my suicide attempt. I finally realized I was allowing emotions to master my life. My feelings of pain and pleasure took over, which took me away from the divine planned purpose for my life. I learned then that I cannot trust my feelings, and my trust must be in God only.

I know what happened when I doubted. I know what happened when I let go of God. I know what happened when I dabbled into other realms that looked and sounded deceitfully the same. Providentially, I found out there is no other name that can bring me to the destination of peace and the land of promise: The name of Jesus.

When you've had so many people lie to you and break their promises, you may lose trust. Even the lies you told yourself and the promises you didn't keep to yourself landed you in doubt, despair, and an attitude of *I don't care*. I know. I was there.

I will not abandon or forsake Him ever again. He was always there for me even when I doubted or denied the truth. I lost hope and faith, and consequently, the spirit of death almost took me out of here.

I am thankful that His ways are better than my ways. That's why I have to say what I'm saying to you. Maybe you don't know what you need to know. What you do with this message is your business not mine. I don't know you, but here's what I know *about you*... You do need the truth and you do need to accomplish your goals, and live your dreams. That's my desire for you as well. Listen to me with your heart and picture all the wondrous things you are meant to do.

I found a better solution and a way out: Love and forgiveness. Who I was then is not who I am now. Decide right now to reclaim your life. We can't undo what's been done, but we can look at it from a different perspective. Forgiveness is not forgetting, it's remembering without anger, shame, or guilt. Let forgiveness be a defining moment. **Forgiveness is freedom!**

Change is necessary; that's life. Behavior modification is temporary. Lasting change comes from a **heart** change. Reference: Luke 6:45 *For the mouth speaks what the heart is full of.*

Take responsibility for where you are now. No more excuses or blame. Accept the consequences for what you say and do. Your old nature and behavior are gone. You must now develop the determination to be responsible and dependable. Always keep your promises and honor your commitments, especially to yourself. Develop your potential. Value yourself. Speak life into yourself. You have the ability to respond differently now.

Let me reiterate how responsibility ties into reinvention. Listen to the words you speak to yourself. If you are accustomed to calling yourself negative names, stop NOW!. (Have you ever seen the Bob Newhart clip, *"Stop It!"* on YouTube? Only watch it if you have a sense of humor.)

No matter how you feel, start complimenting yourself. Look in the mirror and captivate your beauty. Talk to yourself like you would a best friend. What words of encouragement can you speak to yourself? Do it and feel your confidence rise, as you begin to see yourself through new eyes. An even better approach is to write down the scriptures about how God sees you, and speak those words; His words out loud. Fill the atmosphere with loving energy coming from God's Word.

"Feelings are much like waves, we can't stop them from coming, but we can choose which one to surf." ~ Jonatan Mårtensson

RICH - What Does "RICH" Mean to You?

"You are not here merely to make a living. You are here in order to enable the world to live more amply, with greater vision, with a finer spirit of hope and achievement. You are here to enrich the world, and you impoverish yourself if you forget the errand."

~Woodrow Wilson

What does "RICH" mean to you? The first thing that probably comes to mind is money. That is definitely a key meaning of rich but not exclusively. The *love* of money is the root of all evil which leads to temptation causing ruin and destruction. Think about it. People will steal and kill for money. Yes, money does make a difference in your life. You'll soon find out that to have enough money to be comfortable, you've got to be rich. It's then you'll experience comfort. Decide right now to write this down and speak it out, *"I'll never be broke again."*

Zig Ziglar said, *"Money won't make you happy, but everybody wants to find out for themselves."*

Money gives you control over your life, it gives you options, and it allows you to live a life of contribution and give to causes that touch your heart.

There was a book project where authors came together to each write a chapter for *Hunger for the Hustle*. These are stories about how each of us went from struggle to success. I am honored that I was chosen to write a chapter for the purpose of giving value and collectively making a generous contribution from the proceeds to a nonprofit cause, *The Giving Circle,* https://www.thegivingcircle.org/ who are compassionate people helping those in need in Uganda and places near to me like Saratoga

Springs, New York. Their mission is to shape and better lives by building and teaching sustainable solutions in education, health, farming, and economic self-empowerment to end poverty and hopelessness. That is a cause that touches my heart. People working together in love from all walks of life.

Luke 12:34, *"For where your treasure is, your heart will be also."*

No matter where you are in life now, you are already rich. You have the power to increase, whatever that means to you. Even if you are behind on your dreams and behind on your bills, expect to increase your borders to become successful.

Write down specific financial goals. Have an amount in mind of how much money you want to generate and for what purpose. Be dedicated and disciplined, and know it's okay to fail, because failure isn't final.

Put systems and strategies in place. What knowledge and skills do you have that people will pay you for? Master your talents and have faith to act on your dreams. Don't stop pursuing them. When you stifle your gifts, you stifle those around you as well.

"You don't get paid by the hour, you get paid for the value you bring to the hour," Jim Rohn.

When my son was a young boy, he launched his first business. It was a proud moment seeing his budding entrepreneurial spirit in motion. I helped him make fliers about his pooper scooper business. We even wrote a jingle: *"Love your dog but not its doo, let me scoop it up for you."* He loaded up a shovel and bucket into his red wagon that he pulled around the neighborhood serving his clients. Everyone has to start somewhere; you just need to get started. Big or small, you can't win them all, but you will have wins.

Decide on a product or service you can provide that may be valuable to yourself and to others. This service or product could be the means to create wealth. Determine at least three action steps daily. Study who has successfully done what you want to do. Les Brown says, *"You must be willing to do the things today others don't do in order to have the things tomorrow others won't have."*

Now that we've established "rich" requires money, let's see what other factors play a part.

Rita Davenport said, *"Money isn't important, but it's right up there with oxygen."*

Rich is also having a meaningful, enjoyable, happy life despite your circumstances. Rich relationships are essential. Above all else is your relationship with God (not religion), then relationship with yourself and others. Richness is abundance in all areas of your life.

Did you know Jesus was rich? That's right. Many people think he was poor. He had a beachfront property when he lived on earth. How cool is that? I wonder if he had rich, dark chocolate too. Yum!

I remember a story Les Brown told. He said there was a time he was so broke that when he walked by a bank, he'd trip the alarm. Then and now, Les enriches many lives with his stories and messages. Everyone has a story. Your story can add richness to many lives too.

Lives are enriched by enhancing the quality and value of people, even with something as simple as a smile.

RADIANCE - *Let Your Light Shine*

"...and you thought beauty was the outward show – but now you know the truth, My Love – it's always been the inner fire."

~ *John Geddes*

Let your radiance shine. You are beautiful inside and out. Radiance exudes confidence. Radiance is happiness. Radiance shines and lights up the room and others light up too. Radiance is vibrant joy. *"The joy of the Lord is your strength,"* Nehemiah 8:10.

"You're beautiful just the way you are. Shine on. And dare anyone to turn off the lights." -Mandy Hale

If your heart has become hardened, let love in, like *The Grinch* and *Mr. Winter*. I know those are fictional characters, but you get the picture, right?

Let the light of your heart shine through and overflow onto others. Just imagine what a difference you will make. The twinkle in your eyes and the smile on your face will truly light up every place. Speaking life into every soul you meet is a sweet treat.

I remember when I was working in an office with many engineers. There was one guy in particular who was quiet and seemed grumpy. When he gave me work, I drew a smiley face and wrote a cheerful note when I gave him back the finished project. Every day, I greeted him with a friendly hello and big smile. I wasn't sure it made any difference until…

After work one day we sat down to talk. He told me his son just died of cancer. Whoa, no wonder he was down and grumpy. That was devastating. He told me that my notes and kind words uplifted him especially during such a difficult time. That touched my heart.

You never know what people are going through. Like the song *"That's What Friends Are For"* by Dionne Warwick says, *"Keep smilin', keep shinin', knowin' you can always count on me, for sure. That's what friends are for... These words are coming from my heart."* How can you shine and touch the hearts of others?

CHAPTER 4

I = INVEST in Yourself

Bet on You

You must invest in yourself. Warren Buffet was asked the question, *"What's the most important investment you can make?"* The answer was," *In yourself."* Here's a guy with billions of dollars in real estate and billions of dollars in the stock market, who said, *"In yourself."*

Invest in personal development and condition your mind. *Caution: Don't invest your way to broke like I did.* Get return on your investments before digging a huge debt hole. All investments do not require money.

Investing time is always wise, especially time in relationships, starting with yourself and your Creator. It is written in Matthew 6:33, *"But seek first the kingdom of God and His righteousness, and all these things shall be added to you."* In essence, if you **seek** the presence of **God** in thought, word, and deed, the things you require will be given to you.

Hmm… sounds like the true Law of Attraction is found in the Living Word. Now you know the real *Secret*.

Mindset is one key. Another key is having an action plan. Do it and be patient. Action won't produce good results if our beliefs and thoughts aren't in alignment. Therefore, one good recipe is *mindset + action + passion = your desired success.*

Passion creates energy and is magnetic. What are you passionate about? Once you have invested in and believe in yourself, people will see your value. Your compassionate, loving heart will shine through and people will willingly and cheerfully invest in you. Continue to sow seeds of love and keep showing up.

INITIATIVE - *Ready, Set, Go*

"Taking Initiative is a form of self-empowerment."

- Stephen R. Covey

- Initiative requires taking actionable steps.
- Invest in yourself and in your personal growth.
- Do the work required to accomplish your goals.
- Be resourceful and lead yourself well.
- Speak up and share your ideas.

20 seconds of COURAGE -- 3 STEP BREAKTHROUGH PROCESS

1. **READY- Acknowledge what is blocking you.** For example: FEAR, GUILT, or SELF-SABOTAGE; What does that look like? Are you feeling symptoms of fear (anxious, angry, stressed, worried, overeating, or fidgety)? Are you looking for ways to escape the fear?

2. **SET - Set it in its place.** Where is this coming from and why? It may be coming from someone who has their own fears, and they are projecting it onto you. What happens if you give into this fear and you don't go forward with your plan and dreams? What does your life look like? Write it out. (Will you feel guilty that you didn't break through that fear?) What would your life look like if you overcame that fear? (You know in your heart it's the right thing to do. For example, do a Facebook live, or speak on a stage, or write a book.)

3. **GO – Take action steps toward what you want to do.** Don't let the opinions and judgments of others stop you. When you judge others, you are secretly judging yourself. Don't judge, just be you and live the life you were designed to live. Believe you can and speak affirmations (I am strong and can push through). Know difficulties will happen along the way, but it will be worth it.

This 3-step process gets you out of your head, and into your heart and passion.

JOURNAL YOUR THOUGHTS (to the following):

➤ What if you fail?

➤ What if you succeed?

➤ What is your purpose and passion?

➤ What are your natural talents?

➤ What are you not good at and don't enjoy?

➤ What are your next steps?

INTENTIONAL - *Make Things Happen*

"Empty the coins in your purse into your mind and your mind will fill your purse with coins."

-Benjamin Franklin

- Be intentional. See the results already achieved.
- Make things happen; don't wait.
- Focus and eliminate distractions.
- Write down 3 things daily that moves you closer to your goal.
- Know why you want to achieve your goals and dreams.
- You are a valuable investment.

Another defining moment for me was when I intentionally invested in myself and joined a community of people who wanted to improve their communication skills, discover their power voices, and tell their stories. The experience was valuable and was led by the Legendary Les Brown and Jon Talarico. Everyone can benefit from learning to communicate effectively, personally, and professionally. It was a journey of breakthrough, transformation, connections, opportunities, and new friends. Even if you don't know how, intentionally decide to put things in motion. Step by step you'll see progress.

I didn't know how to write or publish a book. I intentionally started by getting the cover created. I proceeded to do the next thing: write something, even when I didn't know all the steps yet. Knowledge, skill, tools, and resources will appear once you are aware and intentional. You can do it, whatever your "IT" is. Seek out people who have already done what you want to do. See how they can help you.

Start by setting S.M.A.R.T. goals: Specific, Measurable, Achievable, Relevant, and Time-bound.

LIVE INTENTIONALLY WITH URGENCY

At any moment, urgent matters may arise. Immediate action will be required. It can throw you into emotional turmoil. You may feel like life is spinning out of control, or…you can put your own spin on it. Choose to transform **urgent** matters into living life with **urgency**. Allow those challenges to awaken a new way and a new you.

Imagine what it looks like beyond what's happening now. See yourself conquering every challenge. Imagine what it feels like to get to the other side and find a way to achieve your goals and dreams.

Sometimes stress and change can knock you down, but don't let it knock you out. This Les Brown quote is worth repeating, *"When life knocks you down, try to land on your back. Because if you can look up, you can get up."*

Your situation may seem impossible, **but God has a comeback for every setback and a new beginning for every ending**. Do you feel like you're in too deep? Being overwhelmed and procrastinating can keep you stuck and scattered. I know, saying goodbye makes me cry. There is loss but you can turn it into a gain, and treasure the moments you shared with people and places. You may feel defeated while you watch others succeed. You are happy for them. For you, maybe you see no way out. What's happening in your life that feels heavy and looks impossible to handle?

Here, with me, you won't get beaten down. This is a safe place. Has anyone ever said to you: *"You're not special,"* or *"It could be worse,"* or *"You're not tough enough,"* or *"You can't do that"*?

I don't know about you, but those words tend to be critical, discouraging and disheartening. Just know that *these individuals lack understanding.*

Let me encourage you and help you get back up with these 6 solutions inspired by the word **URGENT**:

1. **U = UNDERSTAND:** Understand that these are unprecedented times and that whatever has happened may be new to you. You've never experienced it before so it's a big adjustment for you. You don't have to conform, but instead transform. Disregard people who compare or make your feelings seem insignificant. It's significant to you. As I write this, we are living in unprecedented times, and if you add your personal circumstances, it will compound issues. First, just breathe, and be present in the moment. You don't have to figure it all out right now. If one day at a time seems too much, break it down to one minute at a time. Everyone has a different pace. Honor your own pace and don't feel pressured by anyone else. Know that you are greater than your circumstances.

2. **R = REST & REFLECT:** Break. Take a break. Did you think I meant breakdown? That's okay too. Shedding tears is cleansing. It's healthy. Keeping everything inside can be toxic. Handling urgent matters may mean letting go and taking a break from other things for now, even a job. Ask yourself, *"What's most important right now?"* Will you wish you worked more when you look back or when you're lying on your deathbed? Not likely. Take time to take care of yourself. Pushing too hard can lead to burnout and can compromise your immune system. There may be more going on than just emotions. Maybe you need to take a nap, soak in the tub, and eat some good food to refuel and refresh.

3. **G = GIFTS:** Believe. Accept the change and believe it will be okay. Get a new perspective and see the gifts this urgent matter brings. You may experience waves of emotions and face challenges; but

just ride the waves. It's okay. God promises to work everything together for good. Be grateful for the gifts.

4. **E = EVALUATE:** Assess the situation. Explore new possibilities. What can you do to move forward? Where do you want to be? What do you want to be doing? Who do you want to do it with? Picture it in your mind. You don't have to let any situation "*infect*" you and keep you feeling stuck, sad, and hopeless. Allow this new thing to "*affect*" you and transform you into having a better life. You get to choose. Are you living for other people and not living the life you were born to live? You were made for more.

5. **N = NECESSARY:** It's necessary that you work on yourself and develop yourself despite disappointments and setbacks. It's necessary to surround yourself with quality people who believe in you and lift you higher. Remember, when things go wrong, don't go with them, as Les Brown would say. Not just when things go wrong, but when major change happens; give yourself grace to shift into a new gear, adjust your sails, and enjoy the new journey.

6. **T = TRUST:** Trust the process. No matter how it looks now, know the best is just ahead. Take a risk. You don't need to grab the next branch before letting go of the one you're holding onto now. Don't let yourself get buried alive. Don't let your dreams die. Do that new thing that makes your heart sing.

It's **URGENT** that you implement these 6 steps and live life with urgency. No more procrastination, settling, or giving up on your dream and the life you were born to live. No more putting off the passion that burns inside you. Maybe it's writing a book, traveling, starting a business, speaking, creating a new invention, or moving to a different area. What is it for you?

I have a better understanding of "*it's hard but worth it.*" You'll be okay. Get excited and embrace new adventures. We are created for a purpose. Explore where you are now and where you want to be so you can get more out of your life.

IDENTITY - *Do You Know Who You Are?*

- **What does the word "identity" mean to you?** Is it about positive and negative traits, your talents, your strengths, your passions, what you love and care about?
- How do you see yourself?
- What are your core values?
- Knowing your God-given identity gives you confidence, self-esteem, and awareness. You are fearfully and wonderfully made.

I remember being asked to do an exercise where I looked in the mirror and asked myself, *"Who are you?"* The mirror didn't answer that day, maybe it was sleeping.

Knowing whose I am, first reveals *who* I am. I am the daughter of the *Most High God*, who created my innermost being; Psalm 139:13-14 says, *"He knit me together in my mother's womb. I praise Him because I am fearfully and wonderfully made."* You are too. Your identity is in Christ, first and foremost.

The enemy (Satan) does not want you to know your true identity. Philippians 4:6-7, *"Do not be anxious about anything, but in every situation, by prayer and petition, with thanksgiving, present your requests to God. And the peace of God, which transcends all understanding, will guard your hearts and your minds in Christ Jesus."*

YOU ARE A GEM - *A Valuable Treasure*

"You are valuable because you exist, not because of what you do, or what you have done, but simply because you are."

~Max Lucado

When the Queen of Sheba heard about the fame of Solomon and his relationship with the Lord, she came to test Solomon with hard questions. Arriving at Jerusalem with a very great caravan—with camels carrying spices, large quantities of gold, and precious stones—she came to Solomon and talked with him about all that she had on her mind. She found he had wisdom, so she stayed to learn from him. Not only are gems and jewels valuable, wisdom is also a very valuable asset. One is never too old to learn and never too young to teach; though knowing how to teach is a skill.

Each of us has a primary personality. Learning to speak the language of various personalities can enhance communication and understanding. I remember after learning about these "languages," I went to lunch with my dad. It used to frustrate me when he pulled out his pen and wrote numbers down. At that lunch, I finally understood. When he pulled out his pen and scribbled on a napkin, that was how he communicated. Instead of being frustrated, I was able to celebrate and enjoy our time together.

I learned the Gem/color concept from Dani Johnson at a *First Steps to Success* event. Sapphire (blue), ruby (red), emerald (green), and pearl (yellow). Here are typical characteristics of each, which describe a person's temperament or personality:

Sapphires like to have fun and live in the moment. They are spontaneous and spend their money freely. They love travel and adventures. Being outside in the sunshine makes them happy. They like bright things. They have a good sense of humor, like meeting people, and being social. Typically, they are not on time. They are good influencers and promoters.

Rubies like to be first and are motivated by a challenge and by money. They want to win and won't play if they don't win. They are overachievers because they are insecure and need approval from others. They can be abrupt. They like bling and beautiful things. They are confident and get things done. They like to be in the spotlight and get the VIP treatment. They are good leaders and hard workers.

Emeralds are very logical and analytical. They are thinkers and take time to make decisions because they gather data to analyze. They like numbers, facts, and proof. They function best with a precise plan to follow. They tend to be skeptical and often prejudge. They need structure. They don't like surprises and are not spontaneous. They are typically perfectionists and emotionally detached. They are detailed and good at research.

Pearls are kind, personable, and friendly. They are supporters. They are loyal, ethical, and honest. They do not like conflicts or confrontation. They are intuitive and don't like phony people. They are family oriented, love animals and nature. They are peacemakers. They are creative.

These are just brief descriptions. We all have some mixture of all the gems, but there is one primary gem that stands out. Knowing and diving deeper, identifying your own primary gem, and recognizing the gems in others can improve communication in a huge way. This can also improve relationships personally and professionally and get you to know yourself even better.

Gems are valuable and precious. Value yourself and value others and you will shine so bright, you'll need to put on your shades.

INFLUENCE - *Are you being affected or "infected" by Influencers?*

"Never mistake the power of influence."

- Jim Rohn

- Who is influencing you? Are they affecting or "infecting" you?
- Who do you want to influence in an important and impactful way?
- Influencers listen, build rapport, and ask the right questions.
- What powerful influencers have impacted you? Maybe speakers you've heard and books you've read have influenced you in some way.
- Collaborate with those who will work with you to achieve a common goal that will positively influence many.

I want you to think about a person who has influenced your life, and made you feel good about yourself; because of them, your life was never the same.

When I was asked to do that, it took me a while to think of anyone in particular. The part I got stuck on was *"and who made me feel good about myself."* Then, a special aunt and my grandpa came to mind. They were kind, patient, and encouraging. They told me what I was doing right instead of pointing out my flaws and mistakes. I loved swimming in my aunt's pool. It was like going to a country club. She had a slide and diving board. When we got out to soak up some sun, she served iced tea with home hospitality. I remember the kind, caring, enlightening conversations we had.

Then visiting Gramps on his farm was always a fun adventure. I followed him out to the barn to feed the pigs. The pigs snorted and squealed with delight when they got their bucket of slop. Riding with Gramps on the tractor was joyful. He imparted words of wisdom along the way. Many times, not a word was spoken; just watching him and being in his presence was comforting and enriching. I could talk to him about anything. I felt loved, accepted, and appreciated.

Gramps was my mother's dad. Mom told me of a time when she was a young girl, backing up her car in the driveway and backing up into her dad's car. When she told him, he thanked her for letting him know.

She asked, *"Dad, aren't you going to yell at me?"* He said, *"You already feel bad enough about it, don't you?"* Gramps was a patient, understanding, loving man and very funny too.

My dad told me about a time he was helping Gramps bale hay when the tractor broke down. Gramps got some tools to fix it with no success at first. They took a break in the shade and had a cold drink. My dad asked him how he stayed so calm. Gramps told him getting angry wouldn't solve anything or make the tractor run.

Maybe you are having trouble thinking of that person who has influenced your life and made you feel good about yourself, and because of them, your life was never the same. We have been influenced by others somehow, even though it may have been in a critical, negative way, instead of a loving and encouraging way. People may beat us down, but we so often beat ourselves down as well.

An African Proverb says, *"When there is no **enemy within**, the **enemy outside** can do us no harm."* When we let the opinions of others and the opinion of ourselves **negatively** influence us, we can get stuck and *not* step into our greatness. Les Brown says, *"Don't let someone else's opinion of* *you become your reality."* Defining moments can be negative or positive, but either way, our lives were never the same.

Master the skill of building rapport and effective communication. It's not about being friendly and nice, although that helps. It's about connections, showing genuine interest, active listening, and encouragement. Always be learning and stay teachable.

Stand out and stand up by mastering those skills and making your better best.

CHAPTER 5

YOU ARE ENOUGH = *Embrace HIS Greatness*

"God has planted greatness in you. Let today be the beginning of a great adventure as you step into the gifts that He's given you.

~Joyce Meyer

The cover of my first book has a girl sitting on a pier looking out at the ocean. The girl is made up of puzzle pieces with one missing from the middle of her back. That missing piece represents a few factors. One of them being "approval." I saw my life as a series of mistakes that brought pain on myself and the ones I love most. I felt I was being punished and rejected. That produced guilt and shame and self-sabotage. Now I know everything is a learning experience not a bunch of mistakes. I was going in circles and was stuck in confusion and disappointment in myself.

"REJECTION is just Re-Direction. You have outgrown a relationship or place that no longer has the capacity for your greatness." - Dr. Cindy Trimm

How I look at myself now is through God's eyes. I embrace the reality that I am Queen of Hope, co-heir with Christ. I am royalty because I am a child of the Living God, the King of kings. I now look at myself and my circumstances through different lenses. I get to choose and live freely in love, not condemnation. **Continue on your transformation journey.**

STORY OF ESTHER - *Transformation and Transition*

"Every success story is a tale of constant adaptation, revision, and change."

~**Richard Branson**

Our assignments require preparation, training, and practice. Sometimes, however, we may be led in a different direction than we had planned just like Esther, in the Bible. Embrace the hope and courage of her story.

Speaking of Queens and transformation, are you familiar with the story of Esther? She was the cousin and adopted daughter of a Jew named Mordecai. Esther was taken into the king's harem as a young maiden: placed there by divine appointment. From among the harem, a queen was to be chosen. Esther would sit and tell the king stories of the Bible, which were stories about the Jews. Esther was a Jew, but the king did not know it and did not have knowledge or understanding of the Word. When the time came, God gave Esther favor with the king, and she was chosen by King Ahasuerus to be Queen of Persia.

Haman, the king's main prince, hated the Jews, and coerced the king to send out a decree to destroy the Jews... (Esther 3:8-9). The decree was sent out in all the king's provinces to destroy, kill, and cause all Jews to perish in one day... (Esther 3:13). Mordecai reminded Queen Esther that she, being also a Jew, will not escape. He proposed to the queen that she may have been elevated to the palace for that sole purpose of pleading for the lives of the Jewish people... (Esther 4:14). Mordecai asked Esther if she would stand up for her people now that she was Queen of Persia. Esther was faced with the decision of exposing her true identity as a Jew, so as to save her people. She was torn between choosing her people or being chosen by her husband.

Esther acted quickly. She called a three-day fast among the Jews; for at the end of the fast she would approach the king without an invitation. She would have broken that law that said, 'anyone who entered the king's court without an invitation by the king should be put to death; except to whom the king would hold out the golden scepter'... (Esther 4:11)

On the third day, at the end of the fast, Queen Esther walked into the king's court and stood before the king. (You are never to come before the king unannounced). She violated all the rules. When the king saw her, she found favor in his sight, and he extended the golden scepter to her... (Esther 5:2). Her husband did love her. He allowed her to speak as swords were drawn. The king ordered them to put down their swords. He wondered what brought her to this place of desperation to put her life on the line. What was so important to her to make her risk her life? Love covers a multitude of sins. That's how God's word came full circle because they loved each other truly.

Esther loved her calling and God placed her there for that purpose.

She went from a poor Jewish girl to becoming the Queen of Persia and ultimately putting her life on the line to save her people. Now that is major courage and transformation. There is a movie depicting Esther's story called: *One Night with the King*.

The timing and place of your birth are not accidental; God purposely and specifically places us all in certain time frames and places. Many people spend their entire lives never knowing what their purposes are, but perhaps it is because they try to choose their own destiny, rather than following the leading of the Holy Spirit. His ways are better and bigger than ours.

Do what you are placed here to do. You were born for such a time as this, even in these unprecedented times.

What is the desire of your heart? Maybe you just need a different approach and a different way of doing it. Keep pursuing it. God will make a way, just trust Him

SUPPER TIME - *Eat This Bread*

"Jesus has made Himself the Bread of Life to give us life. Night and day, He is there. If you really want to grow in love, come back to the Eucharist, come back to that Adoration."

~ Mother Teresa

RELEASE your faith to RECEIVE God's health and wholeness. How? Partake in the power of holy communion. Say what? Yes. No matter what you believe, hear me out. Ask God yourself (even if you don't believe in God, or you worship some other entity that you call god). I know God saved my life to impart these messages to you. Thanks for listening.

Maybe, like me, you were brought up believing the extreme interpretation that the bread and wine are changed into the real body and blood of Jesus Christ. Those two elements were lumped together believing both represented forgiveness for our sins. The wine represents His blood for forgiveness. The bread represents His body for healing.

The other extreme interpretation is that it is a ritual and needs to be administered by a pastor, priest, or ordained minister. However, you may choose to partake in it yourself as often as you like.

I remember hearing that if you are not worthy, don't come to the communion table. Yikes! *"I better not go."* No, that's not what it means. It's not about your worthiness (that's a whole other topic), it's knowing and honoring the power of the Lord's broken body to bring us health and wholeness. It's not just a piece of bread.

Let's simplify the real significance and true meaning of holy communion. Joseph Prince said that Christians are weak and sick and die prematurely, because we don't discern the Lord's body. When you come to that Table, you must know why. When you take the bread (body of Christ) it means ingesting His health into your mortal body. His body was broken so that yours can be made whole and give you resurrection life.

A 75-year-old woman was lying in a hospital bed after 5 operations. This last operation presented complications. The doctor informed her family to prepare for the worst. The family gathered around their mother's bed in the ICU unit. Placing a crumb of communion bread inside her mouth and a small sip of wine (actually grape juice), they prayed, and all took part in communion together. On the third day, there was a call from the nurse saying to come quickly. Entering their mother's room, they found her awake. Praising and praying, they gave thanks to God. Within a week, that precious woman had all tubes removed and was eating. Soon afterwards she was home and helping her daughter bake cookies. What a mighty God we serve!

Some miracles and healings are instant, and some are gradual. The more you partake, the better and stronger you become. It may sound crazy, but you have nothing to lose and everything to gain. Make a radical change and you will get radical results. RADICAL RESULTS come from taking communion like taking medicine. The good news is God's healing has no adverse side effects. Disarm the enemy! Break his power by proclaiming the Lord's death, which makes all demons flee.

Most people choose to focus on food and exercise as the key to living a healthy life. Yes, the right food and exercise are important; but be sure to also add the essential key of His body, so that your body can receive divine healing and health. God does not want us to put our trust only in natural means to stay healthy.

There are many diets out there. Some people think they will walk in divine health if they are on a Mediterranean diet since that was Jesus' diet. Keep in mind that the people Jesus healed were on that diet as well, but were still sick, because natural solutions can only go so far. The best recipe is to combine eating well and exercise with the Body of Christ.

Trust God. He ordained the holy communion as a channel for his people to have health and wholeness. Break bread with God as you come to His table. No carbs to worry about with that Bread. Experience the power. Receive everything God's Son died to offer you. Holy communion will also add years to your life and life to your years.

Maybe you still don't believe a small crumb can bring you health and wholeness. Think about the Garden of Eden when the forbidden fruit was eaten due to deception. That was what brought sin and disease on the human race. Remember, there is hope and a perfect solution.

Are you robbing yourself of God's source of health, healing, and blessing? I was. It is not a ritual. When you partake, see His loving eyes looking into yours; feel His power and strength filling you up and let Him carry you. Every stripe that He received on His back bears all your struggles, sicknesses, and diseases. Picture all that's been on/in your physical body and see it now on the body of Christ. If you have a tumor, envision it leaving your body and being transferred onto Him. If your heart has been broken, put it on His broken body so that you can receive a new, whole heart. Let Him breathe His breath into you and give you new life.

GET DRUNK - *A Different Kind of Intoxication*

"All you thirsty ones, come to me! Come to me and drink!
~John 7:37

This story started out with me getting drunk and ending up under a truck in a church parking lot. Shocking, right? That was a time I wasn't proud of and was hesitant to share and air my dirty laundry. I decided not to stay in embarrassment and shame, but to be bold and courageous so that my story can help you or someone you know.

I went from wild and crazy, and getting drunk on alcohol and wine for a time, to getting drunk in the Holy Spirit. Now, that was a radical change! Yes, I'm taking you on a wild ride. Hang on! Whether or not you're a believer, this may seem surreal, but it's factual. Take a sip, *"Taste and see that the Lord is good."* Psalm 34:8.

Now I'm telling you to get drunk? *What?* I'm talking about a different kind of intoxication that's out of this world. You may think it's weird, but consider that perhaps it is not the 'drunk in the Spirit' who are weird, but those who aren't.

This "drunken" experience yields great results that will take you higher; versus the other kind of drunk that leaves you down, and possibly depressed in the end. Encountering God is an end in itself.

Some may oppose this experience and won't get it. For those who do, you will experience the joy of the Lord. Joy is not something you can fake. There's a real sense of joy when the presence of God is manifested in that moment. (Psalm 16:11)

When the presence of this joy wells up inside you, your troubles and challenges seem almost silly and insignificant; because you'll know that God loves you like crazy, and that you're not crazy.

I had heard about the baptism of the Holy Spirit but didn't understand it and didn't think I could have it. It wasn't taught to me in my upbringing. Then, God brought me to a new place and gave me this gift. I saw other people receive the gift and thought it was weird at first. *What was everybody laughing about?*

I almost wanted to run out of that place, as I had done so many times before. This time, God had something more that would bring me to a higher level and a deeper relationship with Him and myself. I accepted this gift, but it wasn't activated immediately. I wondered, *"Does this work or not?"*

It wasn't until I got into a quiet, peaceful place alone that the gift was manifested. I paddled my kayak into a private cove on the water with my Bible, journal, and pen. *"Show me how to use this gift, Lord,"* I prayed.

As I kept talking to Him, eventually I heard a language I didn't recognize coming out of my mouth. Whoa! He sure did a new thing in me that day. When I returned from kayaking, I soaked in the bathtub and laughter came over me for no apparent reason. It was a new feeling. I had laughed and been silly before, but this was different. That's when I realized I was drunk in the Holy Spirit and now I could speak in tongues that sounded like *"tie a yellow bow tie"* and other utterances that were foreign.

When you're filled with God's presence, you are in another dimension, the universe of God's love. It is divine happiness. You may want to laugh and shout and dance spontaneously. Those things wouldn't be weird if you were at a sporting event or a concert, right? You just have to let it flow and enjoy the experience of getting drunk in the Holy Spirit.

"Oftentimes, what you wind up learning is very different than what you expect." ~Anne Hathaway

Maybe you'll get drunk in the Holy Spirit, and maybe you won't. I just wanted you to know about it so that you can experience the goodness of His nearness as well. It's powerful! Then you would have access to the heavenlies in the right realm.

His presence is not just a force or a feeling. It is the person of Jesus, with all his emotions and power dwelling inside our weak and frail bodies.

It's an exciting experience when you are laughing with joy because God's Spirit is on you. It's much better to operate out of divine joy than to operate out of the depressing spiritual environment you may be in, especially in these unprecedented times. Back in Jesus' days, and even today, people are desperate to find who they are. They are fighting for significance, survival, and contribution. The answer is in the revelation of what we seek: it is found in Jesus.

There is another Great Awakening happening. It warms my heart to see that many who didn't believe, or rejected this message before, have now accepted and embraced it: those who were afraid to speak out God's name, for fear of "offending" anyone. People are waking up and now realizing the significance of this truth. Some are sincerely stepping out and stepping up to pray openly, even public figures. I say Amen to that. Let us all come together and not be left behind. All are welcome.

May you be moved from living *for* the love of God, to living *from* the love of God. God was pleased with Jesus before He did anything. It's how the Father sees us. Don't base it on the relationship with your earthly father (if you even knew him). Whether that relationship was good or bad, it can't be compared with that of God the Father's.

God, the Father is deeply delighted in us, whether we do or don't do anything. It is the power of the Father's love that truly sets us free. This dynamic is what Jesus wanted to demonstrate to the world. Now that's a demonstration that's worth participating in.

It may sound crazy, but I encourage you to bear whatever cost to experience Him, even if it makes you look like a fool. To the hungry does God reward His presence

CHAPTER 6

YOUR VISION = *See, Believe, Act*

When there is no vision, the people perish.

-Psalm 29:18

Yes, you must picture and see your vision in your mind. Believe it and act on the steps to bring it to reality. The other key piece is, don't give up: PERSEVERE.

PERSEVERANCE is when you want a thing bad enough that you'll go out and fight for it- work day and night for it; and when you feel weary, you'll remember WHY you wanted it.

Let us not become weary in doing good, for at the proper time we will reap a harvest if we do not give up. ~Galatians 6:9

What is that thing you desire? What are you doing about it? What made you stop pursuing it? When I was writing my first book, I put it on the shelf many times. I allowed doubt and fear to creep in. I didn't think it would make a difference. I almost gave up on my dream of being a published author.

Write this down:

1. **Clarify your goals**
2. **Condition your mind**
3. **Celebrate your accomplishments**

I clarified my goal of finishing my book and a stirring rose up inside me. I was reminded that writing that book was a Divine assignment. It wasn't just about me and my story, it was how my story would change and transform many lives. Courage as well as the will to overcome and produce propelled me forward. I took that book off the shelf and I continued writing.

How did I persist and persevere?

I conditioned and renewed my mind with the living Word of God. Those are the most powerful words of all. Also, speaking life into my dreams, reading, looking at pictures, surrounding myself with quality people who already had what I desired, helped to renew my mind.

I also discovered that it took more than why… more than belief and determination. The value and importance that you place on yourself and your goals, are what will put you back in motion. That will produce perseverance. I also remembered that I didn't have to do it alone.

Persevere means "to endure," but there is no sense of having to do it alone. A task or trial is intended to bring you closer to God by showing you that you're not designed to go it alone.

James 1:12 says, *"Blessed is the man who remains steadfast he will receive the crown of life, which God has promised to those who love him."*

I celebrated my accomplishment of finishing and publishing my first book. Now you are reading this book. I kept the momentum going. Whatever you want to accomplish, seek God. Our help comes from the Lord who lives *in* us. The good work He began in you **will** come to completion. Ask the true God to reveal Himself to you, and to come live in you; and watch what happens.

Don't give up on your goals and dreams: persist, persevere, and live your purpose. If you are not clear on what's meant for you, do different things to find out. Each time you do something new, ask yourself if it feels heavy or light? Is it easy and enjoyable? Learn new skills, experiment, have fun.

Here is what I learned writing my books:

- Start before you are ready, don't overthink, over prepare, or get stuck in research.

- Launch your idea and soar where the wind takes you. Don't edit yourself. Let it flow.

- Begin with the end in mind. Create an outline of main points and fill in the details later.

- When panic or doubt hits, that means breakthrough is so close you can taste it. Keep working.

- You are the artist, the creator. Pour your passion and love into your work. Make it come alive.

Time is of the essence. Make your dream come alive now. As my mother used to say: *"Don't put off until tomorrow what you can do today."*

In his speech, **Beyond Vietnam: A Time to Break Silence**, Martin Luther King, Jr. said, *"We are now faced with the fact, my friends, that tomorrow is today. We are confronted with the fierce urgency of now. In this unfolding conundrum of life and history, there is such a thing as being too late. Procrastination is still the thief of time. Life often leaves us standing bare, naked, and dejected with a lost opportunity. The tide in the affairs of men does not remain at flood—it ebbs. We may cry out desperately for time to pause in her passage, but time is adamant to every plea and rushes on.*

Over the bleached bones and jumbled residues of numerous civilizations are written the pathetic words, "Too late."

completion. Ask the true God to reveal Himself to you, and to come live in you; and watch what happens.

Don't give up on your goals and dreams: persist, persevere, and live your purpose. If you are not clear on what's meant for you, do different things to find out. Each time you do something new, ask yourself if it feels heavy or light? Is it easy and enjoyable? Learn new skills, experiment, have fun.

Here is what I learned writing my books:

- Start before you are ready, don't overthink, over prepare, or get stuck in research.

- Launch your idea and soar where the wind takes you. Don't edit yourself. Let it flow.

- Begin with the end in mind. Create an outline of main points and fill in the details later.

- When panic or doubt hits, that means breakthrough is so close you can taste it. Keep working.

- You are the artist, the creator. Pour your passion and love into your work. Make it come alive.

Time is of the essence. Make your dream come alive now. As my mother used to say: *"Don't put off until tomorrow what you can do today."*

In his speech, **Beyond Vietnam: A Time to Break Silence**, Martin Luther King, Jr. said, *"We are now faced with the fact, my friends, that tomorrow is today. We are confronted with the fierce urgency of now. In this unfolding conundrum of life and history, there is such a thing as being too late. Procrastination is still the thief of time. Life often leaves us standing bare, naked, and dejected with a lost opportunity. The tide in the affairs of men does not remain at flood—it ebbs. We may cry out desperately for time to pause in her passage, but time is adamant to every plea and rushes on.*

Over the bleached bones and jumbled residues of numerous civilizations are written the pathetic words, "Too late."

CHAPTER 7

NEXT STEPS
Choose Your Path

Trust in the LORD with all your heart and lean not on your own understanding; in all your ways submit to Him, and He will make your paths straight.

~ Proverbs 3:5-6

Choose a path. I removed what was blocking my growth. I am now creating the life I was born to live. The key is to keep it simple. That may be common knowledge, but not common practice. I tend to overanalyze and overthink things, but I have learned manageable specific steps to the path I was meant to travel.

What are your dreams? Dream big! It can happen. No matter where you are in life now, it's possible. Life doesn't happen to us; it happens for us.

"But I have raised you up for this very purpose, that I might show you my power and that my name might be proclaimed in all the earth" (Exodus 9:16).

Pharaoh mistakenly thought that he was in control. However, God put him in the place of being an Egyptian leader for His purpose. God has a purpose for everyone—including those who resist Him. Ultimately God will get the glory, irrespective of who the person is, because He is the Giver of purpose in every life, whether they live for Him or not.

We are all created for a purpose. What are you called to do? What is stirring in your heart and soul?

Let me drive this point home again: you can be all you were created to be. Believe in yourself. If you don't right now, take my belief in you as a springboard. Stepping into your greatness will not only transform your life, but you will impact many other lives.

Of course, this journey has many twists and turns. That's life. I love this quote by Marilyn Monroe, "*Sometimes things fall apart so that better things can fall together.*"

I encourage you to explore the possibilities. Live *The LORI Factor* way. Take action today because tomorrow is not promised. Your story and your life matter. People are waiting for you.

Where can you go from here?

- Write down the nuggets that resonated with you, now that you've read this book, and create an action plan.

- Discover what I have to offer beyond this book, to assist you on your journey by texting this text only number: 844-394-4798 or email: hello@loribruton.com.

Be filled with joy; the best is yet to come.

I'll leave you for now with a poem to encourage you …

The Bend in the Road

By Helen Steiner Rice

Sometimes we come to life's crossroads
And we view what we think is the end.

But God has a much wider vision
And He knows it's only a bend—
The road will go on and get smoother
And after we've stopped for a rest,
The path that lies hidden beyond us
Is often the path that is best.

So, rest and relax and grow stronger,
Let go and let God share your load
And have faith in a brighter tomorrow.

You've just come to a bend in the road.

www.ingramcontent.com/pod-product-compliance
Lightning Source LLC
Chambersburg PA
CBHW070048120526
44589CB00034B/1596